DK EYEWITNESS TRAVEL

TOP 10

DELHI

GAVIN THOMAS
JANICE PARIAT

Penguin
Random
House

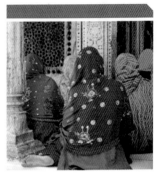

Top 10 Delhi Highlights

The Top 10 of Everything

CONTENTS

Delhi
Area by Area

Streetsmart

Within each Top 10 list in this book, no hierarchy of quality or popularity is implied. All 10 are, in the editor's opinion, of roughly equal merit.

Front cover and spine *Humayun's Tomb, Delhi*
Back cover *The picturesque Lotus Temple surrounded by landscaped gardens*
Title page Spices on sale at a market in Delhi

Welcome to
Delhi

India's buzzing capital is a fast-growing metropolis studded with the remains of ancient empires, where exquisite Mughal architecture, grandiose imperial avenues, dazzling modern temples and pretty little mosques jostle for space amid the city's constant bustle, vibrant colours and evocative scents. With Eyewitness Top 10 Delhi, it's yours to explore.

At its heart is **New Delhi**, the British-built imperial city: elegant and spacious, with fine dining and excellent shopping, bisected by the wide, majestic thoroughfare known as the **Rajpath**. The grandiose 17th-century Mughal city of **Old Delhi**, by contrast, is a warren of teeming bazaars concealing all manner of fascinating nooks and crannies, but its magnificent constructions – the famous **Red Fort** complex and the utterly flamboyant **Jama Masjid** mosque among them – are just as impressive as those of the new city.

South of the centre, the **garden tombs of Humayun and Safdarjung** put into context that zenith of Mughal architecture: the **Taj Mahal** in **Agra**, an easy excursion from Delhi, along with the long-abandoned but architecturally rich Mughal city of **Fatehpur Sikri**. Meanwhile, Delhi's modern, efficient and ever-expanding metro system puts into easy reach the scattered sights of **South Delhi** – most notably the 12th-century **Qutb Minar**, which marks the original location of one of the traditional seven cities of Delhi – before heading out to the satellite towns of **Noida** and **Gurgaon (Gurugram)**, burgeoning IT hubs that crackle with the dynamism of an up-and-coming new India.

Whether you're coming for a weekend, a week or longer, our Top 10 guide is designed to bring together the best that Delhi has to offer, from the hottest Indian cuisine to the most magnificent monuments. The guide has useful tips throughout, from seeking out what's free to avoiding the crowds, plus six easy-to-follow itineraries, which tie together a clutch of sights in a short space of time. Add inspiring photography and detailed maps, and you've got the essential pocket-sized travel companion. **Enjoy the book, and enjoy Delhi**.

Clockwise from top: Taj Mahal, Baha'i Lotus Temple, Qutb Minar complex, Chhath Hindu festival, a spice market near Chandni Chowk, Rajpath, detail from the Red Fort

Exploring Delhi

There are so many sights to see and things to do in Delhi, you could easily spend a couple of weeks here. Whether you're visiting for a weekend or have the luxury of an extra couple of days, these two- and four-day itineraries will help you make the most of your time in this vibrant city.

The Red Fort offers a glimpse into the opulent lifestyle of the city's former rulers.

Two Days in Delhi

Day ❶

MORNING

From **Khari Baoli** market (see p66), take a stroll or a cycle-rickshaw ride down **Chandni Chowk** (see pp14–15) to the **Red Fort** (see pp12–13), before heading over to see the imposing **Jama Masjid** (see pp16–17).

AFTERNOON

Take an auto-rickshaw to the **Crafts Museum** (see pp28–9), then take a short walk to **Purana Qila** (see p93). From there head to **Humayun's Tomb** (see pp18–19) and **Nizamuddin** (see pp94–5).

Day ❷

MORNING

Start at **Gandhi Smriti** (see p79) and from there walk or take an auto-rickshaw to **Safdarjung's Tomb** (see p94). Later, go for a stroll around the peaceful **Lodi Gardens** (see pp30–31).

AFTERNOON

Take an auto-rickshaw along **Rajpath** (see pp20–21) from Rashtrapati Bhavan to **India Gate**, before backtracking slightly to the **National Museum** (see pp32–5). Then get the metro from Udyog Bhawan station to visit the fascinating red sandstone **Qutb Minar** complex (see pp24–7).

Four Days in Delhi

Day ❶

MORNING

See the **Red Fort** (see pp12–13), then pop into the **Lal Mandir** (see p87) and **Gauri Shankar Mandir** (see p88) before walking down **Chandni Chowk** to the **Fatehpuri Masjid** (see p15) and **Khari Baoli** market (see p66).

AFTERNOON

Take a rickshaw to **Qudsia Bagh** (see p88), then check out **Nicholson's Cemetery** (see p49) and the **Kashmiri Gate** (see p49) before heading past

0 metres 1000
0 yards 1000

ritish
esidency

Red
Fort

AUTO-RICKSHAW

1 Crafts
Museum

Purana
Qila

AUTO-RICKSHAW

Humayun's
Tomb

3

Nizamuddin

To Agra,
Fatehpur Sikri
(210 km)

Key
— Two-day itinerary
— Four-day itinerary

The Taj Mahal, Shah Jahan's sublime mausoleum, is a magnificent example of Mughal architecture.

Safdarjung's Tomb features this beautifully decorated arch just above the main entrance.

St James' Church (see p85) and the British Residency (see p48) with a cycle-rickshaw to the **Jama Masjid** (see pp16–17), finishing with a mutton *korma* at **Karim's** (see p65).

Day ❷
MORNING
From **Connaught Place** (see p77), head to the **Jantar Mantar** (see p78), then take an auto across **Rajpath** (see pp20–21) to the **National Museum** (see pp32–5).
AFTERNOON
Get an auto-rickshaw to **Rashtrapati Bhavan** (book ahead, see p21), then

another along **Rajpath** to **India Gate** (see p20) and **Purana Qila** (see p93). Visit the **Crafts Museum** (see pp28–9).

Day ❸
MORNING
Start at the **Qutb Minar** (see pp24–7), visit the **Mehrauli Archaeological Park** (see pp26–27), then take the metro to **Safdarjung's Tomb** (see p94).
AFTERNOON
Visit **Gandhi Smriti** (see p79) before walking around the **Lodi Gardens** (see pp30–31) and going on to see **Humayun's Tomb** (see pp18–19). Head to **Nizamuddin** (see pp94–5) for the evening's *qawwali* session.

Day ❹
MORNING
Take the morning train to **Agra** and visit the **Taj Mahal** (see pp36–7).
AFTERNOON
Get a taxi to **Fatehpur Sikri** (see p39), before returning to Agra in time to catch the evening train back to Delhi.

Top 10 Delhi Highlights

Visitors at the Taj Mahal
in Agra, Uttar Pradesh

Delhi Highlights

History is writ large in Delhi, and few places in the world can rival the city's incredible clutch of monuments, spanning 1,000 years of history. These range from the soaring minaret of the Qutb Minar and the imposing Red Fort to the dramatic Jama Masjid and Humayun's Tomb, as well as some of the most grandiose landmarks of the British Raj, such as India Gate.

Red Fort ①
A former residence of the powerful Mughal emperors, the enormous Red Fort **(right)** is Old Delhi's iconic showpiece attraction, providing a fascinating peek into the cultured world of the country's most charismatic rulers *(see pp12–13)*.

② Chandni Chowk
At the heart of Old Delhi, this famous Mughal thoroughfare, lined with mosques, temples **(left)** and myriad shops *(see pp14–15)*, offers a colourful slice of quintessential Indian street life.

Jama Masjid ③
The largest and most spectacular mosque **(right)** in India, this Mughal monument rises out of the streets of Old Delhi *(see pp16–17)*.

④ Humayun's Tomb
The first of the great Mughal garden tombs **(left)**, this is one of ancient Delhi's most beautiful historical monuments *(see pp18–19)*.

⑤ Rajpath
As the centrepiece of imperial Delhi, this great Raj-era thoroughfare is one of the world's finest examples of Colonial pomp, stretching from the stately India Gate **(below)** to the grand Rashtrapati Bhavan *(see pp20–21)*.

⑥ Qutb Minar Complex

Towering over southern Delhi, the Qutb Minar is perhaps the city's single most dramatic sight, surrounded by monuments from the Sultanate and Mughal periods (see pp24–5).

Crafts Museum ⑦

This engaging museum offers a fascinating snapshot of the myriad local arts-and-crafts **(right)** traditions of the subcontinent, from arcane religious artifacts to traditional village houses (see pp28–9).

⑧ Lodi Gardens

The idyllic Lodi Gardens are dotted with a sequence of atmospheric tombs **(above)** built in honour of the Delhi sultans. The landscaped grounds make them ideal for a picnic (see pp30–31).

⑨ National Museum

The National Museum is India's finest, with an enormous collection of artifacts **(left)** and exhibits ranging from the Harappan civilization to the 20th century, covering every aspect of the country's varied cultural history (see pp32–5).

Taj Mahal ⑩

Perhaps the most famous – and certainly the most beautiful – monument in the world, the incomparable Taj Mahal in Agra **(right)**, a masterpiece of Mughal architecture, never fails to astonish and amaze (see pp36–7).

Map labels:
SHYAMA PRASAD MUKHERJI MG
② CHANDNI CHOWK ①
OLD DELHI
③
SHRADDHANAND MARG
ASAF ALI ROAD
JAWAHARLAL NEHRU MARG
VIVEKANAND ROAD
BAHADUR SHAH ZAFAR MARG
DEEN DAYAL UPADHYAYA MARG
Connaught Place
BARAKHAMBA RD
KASTURBA GANDHI MARG
SIKANDRA RD
TOY MG
FEROZ SHAH ROAD
PANCHKUIAN ROAD
COPERNICUS MG
TILAK MARG
MATHURA MARG
EW DELHI
ATH ⑤
India Gate
⑨
BHAIRON MG
Purana Qila
MOTILAL NEHRU MG
SHAH JAHAN RD
PANDARA RD
DR ZAKIR HUSSAIN MARG
BHARTI MG
RAJ ROAD
SUBRAMANIAM BHARTI MARG
MAHARISHI RAMAN MARG
Delhi Golf Course
HARI PAI PAI LANE
MATHURA ROAD
⑧
ROAD
LODI ROAD
BHISHAM PITAMAH MARG
LALA LAJPAT ROAD
④
BAGH ROAD
8 km ⑥↓
0 metres 1000
0 yards 1000

TOP 10 ⭐ Red Fort

In 1638, the Mughal emperor Shah Jahan (r. 1627–58) decided to leave Agra, then capital of the empire, and return to Delhi. Here he created Shahjahanabad, or Old Delhi as it is now known, with the Red Fort (Lal Qila) at its heart. The structure was completed in 1648 and surrounded by enormous red sandstone walls, their colour lending the fort its name. It served as home to the emperor and his successors until the 1857 Uprising *(see p43)*. Although time has taken its toll, it remains one of Delhi's most absorbing sights.

1 Naqqar Khana
The second of the fort's major gateways, the Naqqar (or Naubat) Khana was where all visitors were obliged to dismount from their elephants to enter the inner court. In the gallery above, musicians would perform in welcome.

2 Khas Mahal
The emperor's lavishly decorated private apartments are divided by a marble latticework screen surmounted by the scales of justice.

3 Hayat Bakhsh Bagh
North of the Moti Masjid lies the Hayat Bakhsh Bagh, or Life-Bestowing Garden, with two small marble pavilions **(below)** at either end, and the pretty Zafar Mahal, a red sandstone pavilion, in a pool in the middle.

4 Moti Masjid
Built in 1659, the Moti Masjid is closed to visitors, though visitors can peer through its latticed marble screens for a glimpse of the delicate courtyard within.

Red Fort

5 Lahori Gate
The Red Fort's main entrance is the majestic Lahori Gate **(left)**, although its original grandeur has been obscured by the bastion added by Aurangzeb (1618–1707), designed to force attackers into a sideways approach.

6 Diwan-i-Khas
This pillared hall is where the emperor would have conferred with his ministers on affairs of state; it was also where Emperor Shah Jahan's legendary, jewel-encrusted Peacock Throne was housed. It remains easily the most lavish building in the fort, with fine marble carving and pietra dura inlaywork.

7 Diwan-i-Aam
One of the Red Fort's most impressive structures, this very elegant sandstone pavilion **(left)** is where the emperor used to hold his public audiences.

THE RED FORT IN THE AGE OF THE MUGHALS

Impressive as it is, what visitors see of the Red Fort today is only a part of the original structure, once a veritable city within a city, with lovely pavilions and gracious courtyards, many of which, sadly, have now vanished. Much of the blame for this falls on the British, who, after the 1857 Uprising, razed many of the fort's grand buildings to the ground. They erected a rather overbearing sequence of barracks in their place which, unfortunately, survive to this day.

9 Shahi Burj and Burj-i-Shamali
The Shahi Burj tower is where water was drawn from the Yamuna River for use within the fort. Aurangzeb later added a fine marble pavilion, called the Burj-i-Shamli, with a water chute leading to a scalloped basin.

NEED TO KNOW

MAP H3 ▪ Chandni Chowk ▪ Lal Qila Metro; Chandni Chowk Metro ▪ asi.nic.in

Fort: 7am–6:30pm Tue–Sun; closed Mon; adm ₹500 (Indians ₹35), video ₹25, audio guides ₹100 plus tax and deposit

Sound and Light Show (English): Feb–Apr & Sep–Oct: 8:30pm, May–Aug: 9pm, Nov–Jan: 7:30pm; closed Mon; adm ₹60–80

▪ Take a break at the café on the premises.

8 Rang Mahal
The centre of the Red Fort's women's quarters **(above)** has carved marble walls, an inlaid marble fountain and the remains of ornate mirrorwork on the ceiling.

10 Salimgarh Fort
North of the Red Fort is Salimgarh, built in 1546 and later used by the British to imprison independence fighters. It now houses a museum.

TOP 10 ⭐ Chandni Chowk

When Shah Jahan built his new city, Chandni Chowk was planned as its principal thoroughfare – a broad, ceremonial avenue leading directly from the Red Fort and a favoured spot for elaborate processions. Most of the street's original buildings are now gone (along with the canal which ran down the middle of the road), but Chandni Chowk, lined with shoebox shops, and eternally bustling with crowds and traffic, retains much of its traditional atmosphere.

1 Gurudwara Sisganj
This large, modern Sikh temple **(above)** commemorates the spot where the ninth Sikh guru, Teg Bahadur, was beheaded on the orders of Mughal emperor Aurangzeb in 1675.

2 Sikh Museum
The museum provides an extremely comprehensive history of the Sikhs in pictures, including some portraits of the ten Sikh gurus.

3 Lal Mandir
Built during the reign of Shah Jahan for the Jain soldiers in his army, the Lal Mandir (Red Temple) is one of Delhi's principal Jain shrines. Made of red Kota stone (hence the name), the temple's towers are major landmarks at the fort end of Chandni Chowk.

4 Town Hall
The elegant British Town Hall **(below)** built in 1864, stands out from cluttered buildings of Chandni Chowk.

NEED TO KNOW

MAP G3 ■ Chandni Chowk Metro

■ The pavements of Chandni Chowk are busy and congested. A rickshaw ride along the road is a fun way to experience this lively area without constantly having to check what's happening up ahead.

■ Halfway down Chandni Chowk is Haldiram's *(see p89)*, good for light meals, or get a tasty *parantha* from the Paranthe Wali Gali *(see p89)*.

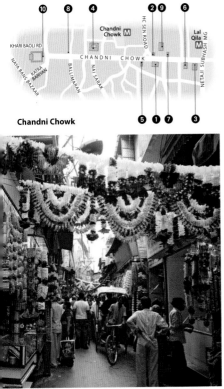

Chandni Chowk

Narrow streets lined with shops in Chandni Chowk

GHANTEWALA

Sadly, Chandni Chowk's most famous sweet shop, Ghantewala, established in 1790, closed in 2015. But sweet lovers won't go hungry, because at the street's western end, Chaina Ram, founded in Karachi in 1901, makes the best halwa in India. Its Hindu owner was forced to flee Pakistan in 1947, but in what amounts to a statement against sectarianism, he set up in Delhi's most Muslim neighbourhood.

⑨ Begum Samru's Palace

Half-buried in the middle of a crowded bazaar just off the main street, this huge Neo-Classical mansion (now occupied by the Central Bank of India), was once one of the grandest buildings in Delhi. It was built back in 1823, and had gardens which stretched all the way to Chandni Chowk.

⑤ Sunehri Masjid

This small Mughal mosque (1721) was named for its gilded domes (*sunehri* meaning "golden"). It was from here that Persian invader Nadir Shah watched his soldiers massacre the city's inhabitants in 1739.

⑥ Gauri Shankar Mandir

Created for Shankar (Shiva) and Gauri (his wife Parvati), this vibrant Hindu temple features an ancient *lingam*, a symbol of worship of the god Shiva; it is said to be around 800 years old.

⑦ Central Baptist Church

The first Christian mission in northern India when it was founded in 1814 (although the current building dates from 1858), this modest church is an atmospheric memento of the Raj era.

⑧ Lala Chunna Mal's Haveli

Built by Hindu merchant Lala Chunna Mal, who had made a fortune supplying British forces in the 1857 Uprising, this sprawling, balconied mansion has no fewer than 128 rooms.

⑩ Fatehpuri Masjid

Located at the far west end of Chandni Chowk, the Fatehpuri Masjid (below) was built by a wife of Shah Jahan in 1650, and has an enormous and wonderfully peaceful courtyard.

🔟 ⭐ Jama Masjid

Completed in 1656, the Jama Masjid (Friday Mosque, named after the Muslim day of prayer) is the largest mosque in India, with three huge domes, a pair of minarets over 40 m (131 ft) tall and a courtyard large enough to hold 25,000 worshippers. The mosque is an architectural masterpiece and took six years to build, using 5,000 masons and at a cost of around a million rupees. Today, its soaring minarets and domes are among Old Delhi's most memorable sights.

1 The Façade
The prayer hall's façade **(above)** is the most impressive of any Indian mosque. Ten cusped arches flank the central *iwan* (main arch), indicating the direction of Mecca and providing a focus of prayer to the many worshippers.

Jama Masjid

2 The Eastern Approach
The most dramatic approach to Jama Masjid is from the east, between the busy stalls of the Meena Bazaar, with the grand mosque looming ahead.

3 Meena Bazaar
This busy market on the eastern approach sells prayer rugs, framed Koranic inscriptions and numerous other Islamic items **(left)**, amid the smoky scent of freshly cooked kebabs from the dozens of nearby *dhabas*.

4 Tomb of Maulana Azad
Halfway along Meena Bazaar, an opening on the right leads up to a raised tomb that houses the remains of Maulana Azad (1888–1958), a major figure in the fight for Indian independence.

5 Prayer Hall

On the western side of the courtyard is the enormous *liwan*, or prayer hall. Its western wall is punctuated by no fewer than seven *mihrabs*, niches that indicate the direction of Mecca to worshippers. A graceful *minbar*, or pulpit, stands to the right.

6 The Courtyard

Designed as a place to go for communal worship, the enormous, breezy courtyard **(below)** has space for thousands of religious worshippers.

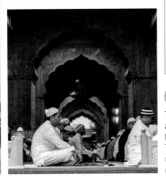

SHAH JAHAN: MASTER BUILDER

Mughal emperor Shah Jahan was a prolific builder, who during his 30-year reign, promoted an architectural outpouring that has never been matched. In addition to Delhi's Jama Masjid and the Red Fort, he commissioned extensive additions to the Agra Fort *(see p38)*, and oversaw a spate of construction in Lahore, Pakistan (including the Shalimar Gardens), not to mention the superb Taj Mahal *(see pp36–7)*.

9 South Minaret Views

The South Minaret affords unrivalled views **(below)** of Old Delhi. There are about 120 narrow steps and not much space at the top.

7 The Minarets

The main prayer hall is framed by two brick minarets. Their slender outlines add a much needed lightness to the long, arcaded façade, which is topped with bulbous Hindu-style *chattris* (pavilions).

8 Pataudi House Mosque

This is one of Delhi's prettiest little mosques – white with triple domes and frilly doorways. It dates as far back as the 18th century, when it was part of a *haveli*, that is now long gone.

NEED TO KNOW

MAP H4 ■ Off Netaji Subhash Marg ■ 011 2336 5358 ■ Chawri Bazaar Metro; Jama Masjid Metro

Open 8am daily until 30 minutes before sunset (at certain times of the day visitors may need to wait for prayers to finish)

Camera ₹200 (female visitors entering the mosque must be accompanied by a man)

■ Visitors are required to dress respectfully (no shorts, short skirts or sleeveless tops). It is a good idea to come with appropriate clothing, although overgarments are provided if needed.

■ There is nowhere to eat or drink within the mosque itself, although the famous Karim's *(see p89)* is close by, and roadside cafés line the surrounding streets.

10 The Domes

Three huge onion domes sit atop the main prayer hall, their bulbous outlines picked out in delicate black stripes. The central dome is partially obscured by the massive *iwan* in front, an architectural conundrum that even Shah Jahan's master architects were unable to resolve.

TOP 10 ⭐ Humayun's Tomb

Built in the 1560s, this gigantic mausoleum is the first of the great Mughal garden tombs and the final resting place of the ill-fated emperor Humayun (r. 1530–40 and 1555–6). The mausoleum is one of Delhi's most impressive sights and a classic example of the great tradition of tomb-building which, almost 100 years later, was to reach its zenith in the Taj Mahal. It is also one of the most peaceful places in Delhi, with a huge expanse of beautiful gardens and an absorbing cluster of further tombs, gateways and mosques.

1 The Western Gateway

The entrance to the gardens is via the western gateway **(left)**. This serves as a kind of architectural curtain, designed to conceal the garden and tomb from the visitor's view until the very last minute, when Humayun's magnificent mausoleum appears in all its glory.

Humayun's Tomb

2 Mosque and Tomb of Isa Khan

The florid octagonal mosque and tomb of Isa Khan **(below)**, a courtier during the reign of Sher Shah Suri (r. 1540–45), provides a complete change of style. Both mosque and tomb lie within their own garden, enclosed in fortress-like walls.

3 The Gardens

The beautiful gardens that surround the tomb follow the Persian-style *charbagh* pattern, in which the garden is divided into four quarters by water channels: a representation of the Islamic gardens of paradise.

4 The Barber's Tomb

According to legend, this elegant tomb was built for the imperial barber – a rather fitting memorial to the person who was trusted to hold a razor to the emperor's throat.

5 Sabz Burj
Housing the grave of an unknown Mughal nobleman, this beautiful blue-domed, Persian-style tomb now stands marooned on a busy roundabout near the entrance to the complex.

8 Nila Gumbad
The striking Persian-style Nila Gumbad, with its blue-tiled dome, houses the remains of an unknown Mughal nobleman.

9 The Tomb
Set atop a large raised platform, the mausoleum is topped by a massive dome. Each of its four façades is dominated by a huge arch.

HUMAYUN

The second Mughal emperor, Humayun, was an endearingly irresolute figure, who alternated between bouts of utter military brilliance and total self-indulgence. After succeeding his father Babur in 1530, he lost his empire to the Afghan invader Sher Shah Suri, and was obliged to seek refuge in Persia for the next 15 years – until he won the empire back. His luck didn't last: one year later he was dead, having fallen down a very steep flight of steps in the Purana Qila (see p93).

6 The Arab Serai
This extensive walled garden is where visiting craftsmen are thought to have lived while they worked on the tomb. It also houses the neat little Afsarwala Mosque and Tomb (above).

10 The Interior
A single door on the southern side opens into the mausoleum's interior (right), where Humayun lies in a small, plain marble tomb.

7 Bu Halima's Garden
The entrance to the complex is through Bu Halima's garden, which has its own gateway. This gateway pre-dates the tomb itself, although the mausoleum and the garden were designed in alignment to it.

NEED TO KNOW

MAP S6 ■ Off Mathura Road ■ Taxi or auto-rickshaw

Open Sunrise–sunset daily

Adm ₹500 (Indians ₹30), video ₹50

■ Walking clockwise around the exterior of the tomb before going inside gives a sense of the scale of the mausoleum. The walk also takes in the Barber's Tomb and Nila Gumbad, after which the tomb can be entered via the southern entrance.

■ There is a pleasant outdoor drinks stall situated in the Arab Serai.

TOP 10 ★ Around Rajpath

Running east to west through the heart of New Delhi, Rajpath (formerly Kingsway) is the grandest of all the city's boulevards, stretching 2 km (1 mile) from India Gate to the presidential palace, Rashtrapati Bhavan. Rajpath was created to showcase spectacular processions and occasions of state, while the surrounding central government buildings were intended to serve as an enduring symbol of British pomp and power to rival – or, indeed, surpass – those monuments left scattered around the city by previous rulers.

③ Cathedral Church of the Redemption

Designed by Henry Medd, assistant to British architect Herbert Baker (1862–1946), this 1935 Neo-Classical church **(left)** was largely inspired by Andrea Palladio's Il Redentore in Venice, and is one of the biggest, most impressive churches in Delhi.

① Secretariat Buildings

Flanking Raisina Hill are the Secretariat Buildings. Designed by Herbert Baker in Neo-Classical style with Indian touches, they now house local government offices.

④ Raisina Hill

The area of Raisina Hill rises between the Secretariat Buildings towards Rashtrapati Bhavan, although the latter only becomes visible once you reach the top, a miscalculation that infuriated Lutyens.

⑤ Rajpath

This grand 2-km (1-mile) axis **(above)** connects India Gate with Rashtrapati Bhavan, linking many of New Delhi's major buildings along the way.

② India Gate

This imposing arch **(below)** commemorates the 90,000 Indian soldiers killed in World War I and the Afghan Wars. Below the arch, the Tomb of the Unknown Soldier honours those who died during the 1971 Indo-Pakistan conflict.

⑥ Sansad Bhavan

Built for the Legislative Assembly in 1935, this distinctive circular building north of Rajpath is now home to the Indian parliament. It is set at a distance from Rajpath, reflecting Britain's grudging attitude towards India's democratic aspirations.

Around Rajpath

7 Mughal Gardens

Set within the grounds of Rashtrapati Bhavan, this beautiful oasis is laid out with watercourses, fountains and neat squares of manicured lawn.

10 Vijay Chowk

Formerly known as the Grand Place, Vijay Chowk is an enormous crossroads marking the point at which Rajpath meets Raisina Hill.

NEED TO KNOW

MAP L3 ■ Central Secretariat Metro & Udyog Bhawan Metro

Rashtrapati Bhavan: 2301 5321 (tours); www.rashtrapatisachivalaya.gov.in/rbtour

■ The main government buildings on Rajpath, which include Sansad Bhavan as well as the Secretariat, are closed to the public. The roads around Sansad Bhavan are also closed, so the Cathedral Church of the Redemption must be accessed from the north.

■ There are a few places to eat and drink along Rajpath, although some of the grassy verges that flank Rajpath, are good picnic spots. The National Museum has a pleasant café in which to relax.

8 Rashtrapati Bhavan

Once the viceroy's residence and now home to the President of India, the magnificent Rashtrapati Bhavan is Edwin Lutyens' masterpiece, a uniquely successful fusion of European and Indian elements. Visitors can register in advance for a guided tour.

9 Military Parades

The Republic Day parade on 26 January **(left)** features a dazzling show of military personnel and brightly coloured floats from every Indian state. Festivities eventually come to a close with Beating the Retreat, a wonderful, ceremonial performance of military bands held on Raisina Hill on 29 January.

Following pages Jama Masjid in Old Delhi

🔟⭐ Qutb Minar Complex

Towering over southern Delhi, the monumental Qutb Minar is one of the city's most dramatic and instantly recognizable landmarks: a triumphal minaret that marked, with a flourish, both the coming of Islam to the subcontinent and the arrival of the Delhi sultans, who held power in northern India for around 400 years *(see p45)*. Further remarkable monuments, including India's oldest mosque, lie scattered at the foot of the minaret and nearby, around Mehrauli village.

2 Iron Pillar

This unusual pillar **(left)**, in the central courtyard, is thought to have been made in Bihar in the 4th century and later brought to Delhi by the Tomars. Remarkably, it has remained rust free for over 1,500 years.

3 Tomb of Imam Zamin

The tomb houses the remains of the Turkestani religious itinerant Imam Zamin (d. 1539) and postdates the Qutb Minar complex.

1 Quwwat-ul-Islam

The first mosque in Delhi, the Quwwat-ul-Islam (Might of Islam), was built by Qutbuddin Aibak (r. 1206–10) in 1192, soon after Muhammad Ghori's conquest of northwest India *(see p42)*.

4 Qutb Minar

Built during the reigns of Aibak and Iltutmish (r. 1211–36), this tapering minaret **(right)** is 72 m (236 ft) tall. A fifth storey, clad in marble, was added later, after the summit was damaged by lightning.

8 Madrasa of Alauddin Khilji
Built around 1317 as a *madrasa* (religious school), this plain building **(left)** has lost most of its original stone facing. Alauddin (r. 1296–1316) himself is thought to be buried in its central chamber.

9 Alai Minar
A large stump of rough stone is all that remains of a rather maverick scheme to build a second oversized minaret, intended to be even greater than the mighty Qutb Minar.

5 Tomb of Iltutmish
Immediately behind the mosque is the tomb of Iltutmish, one of the principal architects of the Qutb Minar complex. Small and plain on the outside, the tomb is lavishly carved within.

6 Alai Darwaza
Built in 1311 as a brand new gateway to the mosque, the Alai Darwaza is richly carved using red sandstone and white marble, a hallmark of the later Mughal style.

Qutb Minar Complex

10 The Prayer Hall Screen
One of the finest pieces of Islamic architecture in all of India, the Quwwat-ul-Islam's prayer hall screen **(left)** is composed of five sharply pointed arches that are covered in Koranic inscriptions and floral decoration.

7 The Central Courtyard
Aibak demolished 27 Hindu and Jain temples to make way for his mosque. The temple pillars were incorporated into the arcade of the central courtyard **(below)**, giving it a Hindu appearance.

THE TOWER OF BABEL, DELHI STYLE
The Alai Minar was the brainchild of Alauddin Khilji, the most brilliant and ruthless of all the Delhi sultans. The plan was to build a minaret twice the height of the Qutb Minar, but the gargantuan project never really got off the ground, and all that remains is a large pile of rubble – "a frustrated tower of Babel", as one writer describes it.

NEED TO KNOW

MAP U3 ▪ Mehrauli, Delhi-Gurugram Road ▪ Taxi, auto-rickshaw or Qutb Minar Metro

Open Sunrise–sunset

Adm ₹500 (Indians ₹30), video ₹50, audio guide ₹100 plus tax and a deposit of ID, credit card or ₹2,000

▪ Arrive early or late in the day to avoid the busy coach parties.

▪ There are drink stalls around the entrance to the complex. For food, it is best to bring a picnic.

Sites around Mehrauli

The beautiful and intricately designed Rajon ki Bain stepwell

 Rajon ki Bain
Built in 1506, this superb *baoli* (stepwell) is atmospherically buried amid woodland in the heart of the park. It has been built up over four levels, with rooms and arcades around the top two floors and a well situated at the bottom.

2 Jamali-Kamali Masjid and Tomb
This beautiful early Mughal mosque, built by the poet Sheikh Fazlullah (known as Jamali; d. 1535), has a delicately carved façade and characteristic red sandstone and white marble stonework. The poet's tomb is located in an enclosure beside the mosque.

Ceiling detail, Jamali-Kamali Tomb

3 Adham Khan's Tomb
Mughal emperor Akbar built this tomb for his foster brother, who was thrown to his death from Agra Fort's battlements for murdering Akbar's prime minister. The tomb's labyrinthine interior has earned it the nickname *bhulbhulaiyan* (maze).

4 Quli Khan's Tomb
Erected for Adham Khan's brother, Mohammad Quli Khan, this neat little tomb was converted into a summer retreat by Sir Thomas Metcalfe. It was christened Dilkusha, or "Heart's Delight"; the ruined walls can still be seen around the tomb.

5 Balban's Tomb
Close to the Jamali-Kamali Masjid lie the fragments of the tomb of Balban (1200–87), one of the most powerful of the early Delhi sultans.

6 Madhi Masjid
Constructed in the early Mughal era, this heavily fortified building looks more like a fortress than a mosque, with a large court-yard and – unusually – two separate prayer halls on either side of a central *mihrab* wall.

 Dargah Qutb Sahib
In the heart of the Mehrauli bazaar (ask locally for directions), this serene little religious complex

honours Qutbuddin Bakhtiyar Kaki (d. 1235), a Sufi saint from Fergana (in modern Uzbekistan), and contains his grave, among other buildings.

8 **Zafar Mahal**
This summer palace was built by Emperor Akbar Shah II (1760–1837) and contains various structures, including Moti Masjid and the tombs of two Mughal emperors.

Sites around Mehrauli

A courtyard within the Jahaz Mahal

9 **Jahaz Mahal**
At the western end of Mehrauli village, this enigmatic Lodi-era structure is thought to have been either a travellers' rest house or an opulent royal pleasure palace.

10 **Mehrauli Archaeological Park**
West of the Qutb, this park was set up to protect the ancient monuments dotted around the area, including over 70, dating from the 11th to the 19th centuries, in the park itself.

METCALFE'S FOLLY

Mehrauli witnessed one of the stranger episodes in Anglo-Indian history when Sir Thomas Theophilus Metcalfe (1795–1853), British Resident at the Mughal Court, decided to establish a summer residence in the area. Rather than build a new house, Metcalfe made the unusual decision to convert the tomb of Quli Khan into an English-style country residence, which he christened Dilkusha (Heart's Delight), although it is generally known as Metcalfe's Folly. The tomb's central chamber was turned into a dining room, a pair of flanking wings and various outbuildings were erected (remnants of which can still be seen), and a string of Indian-style follies were built in the surrounding countryside, including a prominent *chattri* (open-sided pavilion) on a nearby hill. As fate would have it, Metcalfe's love of all things Mughal did him little good: he died slowly, allegedly poisoned by one of the emperor's queens.

The Mughal tomb of Quli Khan

TOP 10 ⭐ Crafts Museum

Delhi's most enjoyable museum showcases India's incredible variety of local artistic and cultural traditions in a rustic building and walled garden designed by Charles Correa (1930–2015). There are some wonderful, fascinating crafts here from every part of the subcontinent and in every medium, from tribal costumes to ivory carvings. There is even a complete miniature village of traditional buildings from across India in the grounds outside.

③ Folk and Tribal Art
This gallery is packed with unusual objects (left) dating from the 19th century to the present day, from a collection of traditional dolls to religious items.

④ Outdoor Exhibits
A number of exhibits are dotted around the Crafts Museum grounds, such as stone carvings from Rajasthan and a striking group of Indo-Chinese statues from Tamil Nadu.

⑤ Cultic Objects Gallery
This gallery houses religious objects from across India, ranging from Hindu bronzes and South Indian paintings to unique Jain and Tibetan Buddhist artifacts.

⑥ Bhuta Sculpture Gallery
Devoted to the Bhuta cult of Karnataka, this gallery (left) contains images from the shrine of Nandikeshvara in Udipi province, carved in dark jackfruit wood and featuring striking human and animal-headed figures.

① Museum Building
Designed by Indian architect, Charles Correa, this rustic ochre-coloured building, encircled by shady verandahs and set in a tree-filled compound, feels like a rural village in the heart of Delhi.

② Resident Craftspeople
The small courtyard, at the back of the museum, is home to a selection of stalls. Artisans can often be seen at work on a wide range of crafts, such as painting, stone carving, metalworking and weaving. They also sell their products.

NEED TO KNOW
MAP R3 ■ Bhairon Marg ■ 233 71370 ■ Pragati Maidan Metro

Open 10am–5pm Tue–Sun

■ The museum is a good place to shop for crafts, but it pays to do some research beforehand. It is usually best to visit the government emporiums around Connaught Place to see what is available and get an idea of prices.

■ Permission to take photographs can be obtained from reception.

■ Visit Café Lota, inside the museum. It is popular for serving fusion Indian cuisine and a variety of teas and coffees.

8 Traditional Buildings

Scattered around the museum garden is a fascinating collection of traditional buildings from across India, including a a traditional house **(left)** from Kullu in the state of Himachal Pradesh.

GALLERY GUIDE

The Crafts Museum is relatively small and can be covered in a couple of hours. All the galleries are laid out over the ground floor of the building, except the Textile Gallery and a section of the Courtly Crafts Gallery, which are tucked away upstairs and can be easy to miss.

7 Textile Gallery

Key to Floorplan
▦ Ground floor
▨ First floor

10 Courtly Crafts Gallery

10 Courtly Crafts Gallery

5 Cultic Objects Gallery

2 Resident Craftspeople

3 Folk and Tribal Art

1 The Museum Building

9 Shopping for Crafts

8 Traditional Buildings

6 Bhuta Sculpture Gallery

7 Textile Gallery

This beautiful, well-curated gallery provides an overview of India's textile traditions, with a vast collection of fabrics in styles including brocade, block printing, tie-dye and appliqué.

9 Shopping for Crafts

The museum has one of Delhi's most interesting selections of traditional crafts for sale, either from one of the stalls at the back of the museum **(below)**, or the shop.

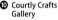

10 Courtly Crafts Gallery

Aristocratic arts from the 18th century to today are displayed here, including *bidri*-ware (silver inlay work) **(above)**, enamelware, jade, ivory carvings and glass jewellery.

TOP 10 ⭐ Lodi Gardens

One of the most enjoyable excursions in Delhi, the beautiful Lodi Gardens offer a winning combination of nature and history. The gardens themselves are among the most attractive and relaxed in the city, with quiet paths winding between tropical trees and plentiful birdlife in the branches overhead. The series of fine medieval tombs dotted among the trees and lawns, erected by nobles of the Lodi and Sayyid Dynasties during the later years of the Delhi Sultanate, provide historical interest.

2 Muhammad Shah's Tomb

The tomb of Sayyid ruler Muhammad Shah (r. 1434–44) is built in the octagonal shape favoured by the later Delhi sultans, its main dome surrounded by eight small *chattris* **(left)**.

1 Sikander Lodi's Tomb

At the northern end of the gardens is the tomb of Sikander Lodi (r. 1489–1517), the penultimate Delhi sultan. It occupies an idyllic garden and has interior walls that feature the remains of the original blue tilework.

3 The Gardens

The gardens were created in 1936 by Lady Willingdon, wife of the viceroy and governor-general of India. She had the two villages that formerly stood here demolished to make way for the new gardens.

THE SAYYID AND LODI DYNASTIES

The Sayyid and Lodi Dynasties held sway from 1414 until 1526, though their power was challenged by a series of internal rebellions and external threats. The first Sayyid sultan, Khizr Khan, rose to power after Timur's invasion in 1398; while the last sultan, Ibrahim Lodi (r. 1517–26), was killed by Timur's great-great-great-grandson, Babur, who was the founder of the Mughal Dynasty.

4 National Bonsai Garden

Near the southern entrance to the park, the National Bonsai Garden sports a collection of tiny trees. A few displays show the various styles of traditional bonsai.

5 Athpula

Located near the tomb of Sikander Lodi, the striking, graceful Athpula (Eight Piers) bridge **(above)** was built during the reign of Mughal emperor Akbar (r. 1556–1605).

6 Shish Gumbad
Built around 1600 for an unidentified nobleman, this is a cuboid-shaped tomb (below), enlivened with bands of rich blue tiles, which run around the middle and top.

8 Bara Gumbad Masjid
Attached to the Bara Gumbad Tomb, this mosque is small but lavishly decorated, with swirls of Koranic script (right) covering every available surface.

Lodi Gardens

7 Birdlife
The gardens are home to a rich array of birdlife, including tree pies, blue throats, spotted owlets, geese and green parakeets (right).

9 Round Tower
To the east of the Bara Gumbad stands a solid-looking round tower, probably built during the 14th century.

10 Bara Gumbad Tomb
Dating from around 1500, the Bara Gumbad Tomb is the gardens' most impressive structure, a cuboid tomb (occupant unknown), topped by a massive dome. Its rather severe outlines are relieved by alternating panels of red and black stone.

NEED TO KNOW

MAP N6 ■ Lodi Road
■ Taxi, auto-rickshaw or Jor Bagh Metro

Open Apr–Sep: 5am–8pm daily; Oct–Mar: 6am–8pm daily

■ There is nowhere to eat or drink within the gardens, but just beyond the southeast corner, Lodi Garden Restaurant (3310 5163) offers refreshments in a lovely outdoor setting.

■ The India Habitat Centre, near the southern entrance on Lodi Road, has a couple of attractive cafés.

TOP 10 ★ National Museum

Founded in 1949, the superb National Museum is India's finest, with a collection of over 200,000 exhibits charting five millennia of subcontinental history. Every major strand in India's complex cultural identity is covered here, with artifacts from across the country and beyond, including prehistoric archaeological finds, Buddhist statues, Chola bronzes and Mughal miniatures.

1 Mughal Emperor Shah Jahan in Dara Shikoh's Marriage Procession

Painted around 1750 in Awadh, this painting **(below)** is a good example of superbly detailed Indian miniature art, portraying the wedding procession of Shah Jahan's favourite son, Dara Shikoh.

4 Dancing Girl

This small but famous image of an elegant, long-legged dancing girl **(left)** was found in Mohenjodaro. Dating from around 2500 BC, it is one of the world's oldest cast-bronze statuettes.

2 Harappan Bronze Chariot

One of the museum's most charming pieces is a bronze figurine (c. 2000 BC) of a man on a chariot pulled by oxen.

5 Ganga

This 5th-century Gupta terracotta statue is one of the museum's most graceful. The river goddess Ganga is seen walking on the back of her mythical animal mount, the crocodile-like *makara*, whilst carrying an urn **(below)**.

3 Avalokitesvara

These rare 9th- and 10th-century silk paintings, from the town of Dunhuang on the old Silk Route in north-western China, depict Avalokitesvara, the Bodhisattva of Infinite Compassion, a deity of Vajrayana Buddhism.

NEED TO KNOW

MAP N3 ■ 11 Janpath, just south of Rajpath ■ 2301 9272 ■ Udyog Bhawan Metro ■ www.nationalmuseumindia.gov.in

Open 10am–5pm Tue–Sun; closed on public holidays

Adm ₹650 (Indians ₹20), audio guide free with a deposit of ID, credit card or ₹2,000 (Indians ₹150 for an English audio guide)

■ The museum regularly closes areas or galleries for renovation. It is best to call ahead or check the website first.

■ The collection is huge, so don't try to see everything at once. An audio guide picks around 30 of the best exhibits.

■ The film show runs Tue–Sun at 11:30am, 2:30pm and 4pm.

■ There is a small café on the museum premises.

GALLERY GUIDE

The museum collection is arranged over three floors, although almost all of the best exhibits are to be found on the ground floor of the building. The first nine exhibits described here are displayed on the ground floor, while the tenth is on the first floor. The museum's film show on Art and Culture is a must-see. Near the museum's reception area, there is also a shop, with books and replicas of some of the exhibits for sale. A visit to the extensive library can be valuable for researchers.

7 Shiva Nataraja
This iconic 12th-century Chola bronze (left) shows Shiva as *nataraj* ("lord of the dance"), surrounded by a ring of fire, representing the cycle of life. He is performing *tandava*, the cosmic dance of destruction and creation.

6 Mughal Nativity Painting

This Muslim version of a usually Christian subject (below) may seem surprising, but Jesus is revered as a prophet by Muslims, and Mary is mentioned more in the Koran than in the Bible.

8 Baluchari Sari
Rare 18th-century silk saris with delicate floral patterns are part of the collection. They were made in Murshidabad (West Bengal), one of the country's most famous silk production centres.

10 Kali
The fearsome goddess Kali, one of the more favoured deities of the Cholas, appears serenely poised and unusually benign in an outstanding late 12th-century bronze.

Asita's Visit to Suddhadhana 9

This is a beautifully carved stone bas-relief (right) from the great Satavahana-era Buddhist monastery of Amaravati (Andhra Pradesh), dating from the 1st–2nd century AD. The panel depicts the sage Asita visiting King Suddhadhana in the town of Lumbini to admire his son, the newly born Buddha.

National Museum Collections

Key to Floorplan
  Ground floor
  First floor
  Second floor

1 Kushan (Gandhara, Mathura and Ikshavaku Art)

This superb collection of classical sculpture from the Gandhara kingdom (in Afghanistan) is famous for its remarkable Indo-Greek culture, in which local Buddhist traditions intermingled with the Greek styles brought to the region by Alexander the Great (356–23 BC).

2 Gupta Terracotta and Early Medieval Art

The classic art of the Guptas (3rd–5th centuries), the second of India's great dynasties, is on show here, alongside some of the more flamboyant statues from the early Pallava (300–900 AD) and Chola (300 BC–1279 AD) kingdoms of the south, featuring beautiful, intricately carved Hindu gods.

3 Bronzes

This is one of the museum's highlights: a room full of Chola bronze statues of Hindu deities, including one of the most iconic images of Indian art – a pair of Shiva *natarajas*.

4 Late Medieval Art

Outstanding examples of the sculptural arts that flourished across central and southern India during the 11th and 12th centuries feature in this excellent collection, including those from the Vijayanagar, Hoysala, Chola and Pala kingdoms.

5 Harappan Civilization

The museum is one of the world's finest showcases of artifacts from the Harappan (or Indus Valley) Civilization (circa 2500–1500 BC). On display are a wide range of finds from Harappa, Mohenjodaro and elsewhere, vividly bringing one of the world's most ancient cultures to life.

6 Indian Miniature Paintings

Another of the museum's highlights, this is an extensive collection of superbly detailed and vibrant paintings from the schools of Rajasthani, Pahari, Deccani and Mughal.

7 Maurya, Sunga and Satavahana Art

These galleries are devoted to the art of the Mauryans (321–185 BC), India's first great empire, and their successors. Displays include monumental sculptures, bas-relief carvings and stone pillars, most

Sunga sculpture of an amorous couple

INDIAN MINIATURE PAINTING

Although originally of Persian origin, the art of the miniature was perfected in India, where artists developed a distinctive style of brilliantly coloured and minutely detailed painting, usually depicting either religious subjects or scenes from courtly life. Miniature painting flourished under Muslim patronage throughout India – the Mughals, in particular, commissioned thousands of pictures and illustrated manuscripts, while distinctive regional schools subsequently developed in Rajasthan, the Deccan and across the Pahari region in the Himalayan foothills. Most artists remain anonymous, although a few of the most famous are listed on the right.

TOP 10 MINIATURE PAINTERS

1 Mir Sayyid Ali (Persian/ Mughal, 16th century)

2 Abd al-Samad (Persian/ Mughal, 16th century)

3 Basawan (Mughal, 16th century)

4 Mansur (Mughal, 17th century)

5 Bishandas (Mughal, 17th century)

6 Abu al-Hasan (Mughal, 17th century)

7 Govardhan (Mughal, 17th century)

8 Bichitr (Mughal, 17th century)

9 Sahibdin (Rajasthan, 17th century)

10 Dalchand (Rajasthan, 18th century)

Miniature painting (1750) from Bundi, Rajasthan, depicting ladies playing *chaupar*, National Museum

recovered from Buddhist temples, including panels from the Buddhist monastery of Amaravati in Andhra Pradesh *(see p33)*.

8 Decorative Arts and Textiles

Dedicated to India's rich and varied clothing and textile traditions, this gallery features a colourful display of woven, printed, tie-dyed, embroidered and appliqué-worked fabrics in silk, cotton and wool. Examples of India's varied decorative arts, including exquisite artifacts made from ivory, jade, glass, ceramic and wood, fill the adjoining galleries.

Silver-incised bowl, Decorative Arts Gallery

9 Tribal Lifestyle

This is a rare glimpse into the lives of India's little-known, Chinese-descended north-eastern tribes. Exhibits include simple weapons, household items and some unusual headgear, backed up by fascinating black-and-white photos of tribes in traditional attire.

10 Buddhist Art

A wide range of Buddhist art and arti-facts from across India, Nepal, Gandhara and China are on display here, including some rare *thangkas* (devotional paintings), statues and a pair of fine silver-and-brass temple trumpets from Ladakh.

TOP 10 ★ Taj Mahal, Agra and Fatehpur Sikri

In 1504, Sikandar Lodi moved his capital from Delhi to Agra. Shah Jahan moved it back in 1638, but when his favourite wife – Mumtaz (or "Taj") Mahal – died before the move, the grief-stricken emperor had this magnificent tomb built for her in Agra. Of unparalleled beauty, the Taj is the zenith of Mughal architecture. Agra has other wonderful Mughal structures, and just down the road, Shah Jahan's grandfather, Akbar, had an entire city built at Fatehpur Sikri.

4 The Tomb

The Taj Mahal's classic perfection is rooted in the simplest of architectural concepts. The main tomb is a perfect cube, while the dome itself is of equal height to the building on which it rests.

1 The Charbagh

The Taj sits at the far end of one of the finest Mughal *charbagh*-style gardens **(above)**, an expanse of lawn divided into four by raised marble water channels.

5 The Dome

The dome rises to a height of 73 m (240 ft), topped by a lotus-shaped design and surrounded by four smaller *chattris* (domed pavilions), echoing those that cap the four minarets.

2 Chowk-i-Jilo Khana

The Chowk-i-Jilo Khana is a forecourt. At its northern edge is a gateway, which leads to the Taj but screens it from the view of those outside.

6 Minarets

Minarets mark each of the four corners. Unusually, these are detached from the main tomb, so that if any of them ever fell, they would collapse away from the main tomb.

7 The Lotus Pool

The centre of the *charbagh's* four intersecting water channels is marked by the marble Lotus Pool, symbolizing the pool in the Islamic gardens of paradise.

3 Tomb Chamber

The tomb of Mumtaz Mahal **(below)** sits at the centre of the atmospheric tomb chamber, and is protected by an exquisitely detailed *jali* (carved screen), while the tomb of Shah Jahan lies alongside it.

8 Calligraphic Panels

Koranic inscriptions frame the tomb's four archways. The script in the higher panels has been enlarged to compensate for the distorting effects of perspective.

⑨ Mosque and Mehman Khana

The Taj is flanked by two mirror-image buildings: a mosque **(above)** and the Mehman Khana, or *jawab* (response). The *jawab* cannot be used for worship since it is oriented the wrong way round.

Taj Mahal, a masterpiece of unparalleled beauty

Taj Mahal

NEED TO KNOW

MAP C3

Taj Mahal: Taj Ganj, Agra, 215 km (134 miles) SE of Delhi; 6am–7pm Sat–Thu; adm ₹1000 (Indians ₹40)

Fatehpur Sikri: 45 km (28 miles) SW of Agra; sunrise–sunset daily; adm ₹260 (Indians ₹20), video ₹25, audio guide ₹100 plus tax and deposit of ID or ₹2,000 (the Jama Masjid and the museum are free to enter)

▪ Arrive early at the Taj to avoid the crowds. Security is tight and visitors are not allowed to bring in food, drink (apart from a bottle of water), phones or even guidebooks. There are a number of cafés outside in Taj Ganj.

▪ Fatehpur Sikri's small Archaeological Museum (9am–5pm Sat–Thu) displays artifacts dating from before Fatehpur Sikri was built.

⑩ Pietra Dura

Large parts of the Taj Mahal's exterior walls are covered in excellent pietra dura inlay **(above)**, in which intricate stylized geometrical floral patterns are created using coloured precious and semiprecious stones.

Sights in Agra

 Sikandra
MAP C3 ■ Open sunrise–sunset daily ■ Adm

The huge mausoleum of Sikandra is one of the grandest of all the Mughal monuments, although something of an architectural hotch-potch, with the usual rooftop dome replaced with a strange four-storey pavilion.

The tomb of Akbar, Sikandra

2 Taj Nature Walk
MAP C3 ■ Open 9am–6:30pm daily ■ Adm

This is an attractive area of wooded parkland, with views of the Taj itself.

3 Mehtab Bagh
MAP C3 ■ Open sunrise–sunset daily ■ Adm

The Moonlight Garden offers the ultimate view of the Taj Mahal.

4 Itimad-ud-Daulah
MAP C3 ■ Open sunrise–sunset daily ■ Adm

Built by Nur Jahan (1577–1645), this tomb is modest in size but exquisitely decorated with pietra dura.

5 Agra Fort
MAP C3 ■ Open sunrise–sunset daily ■ Adm and charge for video

The Agra Fort was originally built by Akbar (1542–1605) and enlarged and embellished by Jahangir (1569–1627) and Shah Jahan.

6 Jama Masjid
MAP C3 ■ Open sunrise–sunset daily

Built in 1648, this spectacular mosque, topped with a trio of domes, is a perfect example of the late-Mughal architectural style perfected during the reign of Shah Jahan.

7 Kinari Bazaar
MAP C3 ■ Open 11:30am–6pm Mon–Sat

This atmospheric bazaar is home to the city's purveyors of *petha*, an unusual confection made from crystallized pumpkin.

8 Chini-ka-Rauza
MAP C3 ■ Open daily

This Persian-style tomb (1628-39) was built for Afzal Khan, a poet who served as Shah Jahan's minister.

 Rambagh Gardens
MAP C3 ■ Open sunrise–sunset daily ■ Adm

These formal gardens are laid out in the traditional Persian *charbagh* plan.

10 Mariam's Tomb
MAP C3 ■ Open sunrise–sunset daily ■ Adm

This pretty tomb was built in honour of Mariam Zamani, one of Akbar's wives and mother of Jahangir.

Itimad-ud-Daulah

Sights in Fatehpur Sikri

Visitors outside the impressive Jama Masjid (Dargah Mosque)

1 Jama Masjid (Dargah Mosque)

The magnificent Jama Masjid, one of the biggest mosques in India, houses the tomb of the Sufi saint Salim Chisti. It is entered through a massive, spectacular gate called the Buland Darwaza, which leads into the mosque's huge courtyard.

2 Diwan-i-Aam

The emperor received ordinary subjects in this courtyard, whose colonnade is topped with Hindu-style capitals. The emperor sat in a small pavilion flanked by carved screens.

3 Diwan-i-Khas

The emperor's private audience hall deliberately combines Muslim, Hindu, Buddhist and Christian features.

4 Hiran Minar

Just outside the city to the north, the odd-looking Hiran Minar is a beacon tower said to be built over the grave of Akbar's favourite elephant.

Hiran Minar

5 Pachisi Court

In the palace's main courtyard there is a giant outdoor board for *pachisi*, the original version of ludo. Akbar would play here using colourfully dressed servant girls as live pieces.

6 House of the Turkish Sultana

The "Turkish sultana" (one of Akbar's wives) probably didn't live in this little pleasure pavilion. More correctly, it is called the Anup Talao Pavilion, after the adjacent small square pool with a stage in the middle.

7 Daulat Khana

Akbar's private quarters have three parts. The library once housed his collection of over 25,000 manuscripts. The room behind it was his study, and upstairs was his bedroom, known as the *khwabgah*.

8 Panch Mahal

The "five-storey palace" narrows with each successive floor and marks the beginning of the *zenana* or women's quarters. Its columns originally had screens between them, shielding the women from view.

9 Sunehra Makan

Akbar's mother may have lived in the "golden house". Its interior murals, although sadly faded, are still impressive.

10 Jodhabai's Palace

The main harem was home to Akbar's senior wives (he had 13 wives in all). It is a grand affair, modelled on the ornate palaces of Hindu Rajput princes.

The Top 10
of Everything

**Muslim women praying at the
shrine of Nizamuddin**

🔟 Moments in History

The citadel of Qila Rai Pithora

① AD 736: Founding of Delhi

Delhi was founded by the Rajput Tomars in the Surajkund area, south of the modern city. In 1060, the town was relocated 10 km (6 miles) west by Tomar ruler Anangpal II, who created a new fortified citadel there called Lal Kot. Around 1160, the Tomars became vassals of the Chauhans, another Rajput clan from Ajmer, who extended Lal Kot and renamed it Qila Rai Pithora.

② 1192: Founding of the Delhi Sultanate

Muhammad of Ghori, from Ghazni (Afghanistan), invaded north India in 1191, but was defeated by Prithviraj Chauhan III at the Battle of Tarain. A year later, Muhammad returned, defeated Prithviraj and took control of northern India. He went home, leaving Qutbuddin Aibak, his general, in charge of Delhi. Aibak became the first sultan of Delhi following Muhammad Ghori's death in 1206.

③ 1327: To Daulatabad and Back Again

Muhammad bin Tughlaq moved the capital from Delhi to Daulatabad (present-day Devagiri), 1,500 km (932 miles) to the south. Delhi's entire population was forcibly relocated to the new city. Daulatabad, however, lasted only two years before Tughlaq abandoned it and returned to Delhi.

④ 1398: Invasion of Timur

A Mongol army led by Timur the Lame, or Tamerlaine as he is better known in the West, sacked Delhi and left it in ruins, leading to the fall of the Tughlaq Dynasty.

⑤ 1526: Arrival of the First Mughals

Babur, a Central Asian adventurer and former ruler of Fergana, Kabul and Samarkand, defeated the last Delhi sultan, Ibrahim Lodi, at the Battle of Panipat (1526) and ushered in the Mughal Dynasty.

Artwork depicting Babur in Kabul

⑥ 1638: Foundation of Shajahanabad

The fifth Mughal emperor, Shah Jahan, transferred India's capital from Agra (where it had been moved by his predecessor, Akbar) back to Delhi. Once there, he founded the brand new city of Shahjahanabad, or Old Delhi, as it is known today.

A depiction of the 1857 Uprising

7 1857: Indian Uprising

In 1857, Indian soldiers across north India revolted and seized control of major cities which were under British control, including Delhi, Lucknow and Kanpur. Delhi became the focus of the movement, as the sepoys rallied behind the Mughal emperor, Bahadur Shah Zafar II. The rebellion was quelled and the conflict stopped after months of bitter fighting. Not long afterwards, the city of Delhi was retaken by the British.

8 1911: Foundation of New Delhi

The capital of British India was moved from Calcutta to Delhi and work began on building the grandiose city of New Delhi under the creative leadership of Edwin Lutyens. The city was inaugurated in 1931 – ironically, the same year the British agreed, in principle, to grant India its independence at a future date.

9 1947: Independence

India was partitioned and became independent. Delhi lost a large proportion of its former Muslim population, while huge numbers of Hindu and Sikh refugees from Pakistan arrived in their place, decisively changing the city's cultural and demographic constitution.

10 1984: Assassination of Indira Gandhi

The assassination of Prime Minister Indira Gandhi (1917–84) by two of her Sikh bodyguards was followed by citywide rioting. Thousands of Sikhs were killed by lynch mobs and their homes were set on fire.

TOP 10 HISTORICAL FIGURES

1 Qutbuddin Aibak
The Turkish slave General Qutbuddin Aibak (1150–1210) founded the Delhi Sultanate, which eventually saw 36 rulers from five separate dynasties control this region of north India.

2 Razia Sultan
Female sultan Razia (r. 1236–40) broke every gender stereotype of her time, appearing unveiled in public and going into battle on horseback.

3 Alauddin Khilji
Alauddin (r. 1296–1316) was perhaps the most brilliant – and certainly the most ruthless – of the Delhi sultans.

4 Muhammad bin Tughlaq
The second Tughlaq ruler (1300–51), was responsible for building the fourth city of Delhi, named Jahanpanah.

5 Sher Shah Suri
This formidable Afghan adventurer (1486–1545) wrested power from the second Mughal emperor, Humayun.

6 Shah Jahan
The sublime Taj Mahal was built by this Mughal emperor (1592–1666).

7 Bahadur Shah Zafar II
The last Mughal emperor, Bahadur Shah Zafar II (1775–1862), was the figurehead of the 1857 Uprising.

8 Mirza Ghalib
Ghalib (1797–1869) was the Urdu language's greatest poet, known particularly for his *ghazals* (see p63).

9 Edwin Lutyens
This British architect (1869–1944) designed much of New Delhi.

10 Mohandas K Gandhi
The eminent leader (1869–1948) of the Indian independence movement was assassinated in Delhi.

Mohandas K Gandhi

🔟 Delhi Sultanate Sights

The modest tomb Lal Gumbad

1 Lal Gumbad
MAP V2 ■ Panchsheel Park South, off Gamal Abdel Nasser Marg ■ Hauz Khas Metro ■ Open 24 hrs

Built for local Sufi saint Kabiruddin Aulia in 1397, the Lal Gumbad is very similar to the earlier tomb of Ghiyasuddin Tughlaq – a cube of red sandstone, almost devoid of extraneous decoration. This is Tughlaq architecture at its most austere.

2 Hauz Khas
Hauz Khas & Green Park Metro

The lake in Hauz Khas was built by Alauddin Khilji in 1304 to supply water to his new city at Siri. Most of the pavilions around it were added half a century later by Feroz Shah Tughlaq, who is buried here.

3 Begumpuri Masjid
MAP V2 ■ Begumpur, off Guru Govind Singh Road ■ Hauz Khas Metro

The finest of the various Sultanate-era mosques

scattered about the city, the Begumpuri Masjid is a perfect example of the austere and monumental style favoured by the Tughlaq Dynasty. The simple mosque is raised, fortress-like, above the surrounding streets, centred on a huge courtyard, with a massive gateway above the central prayer hall.

4 Tomb of Ghiyasuddin Tughlaq
MAP X3 ■ Tughlaqabad ■ Tughlaqabad Metro

This simple, yet striking, red tomb is the final resting place of one of medieval India's most powerful rulers, Ghiyasuddin Tughlaq. The tomb is an almost windowless structure with sloping sides set within a small fortified compound.

5 Lodi Gardens
The delicately constructed octagonal tombs of Muhammad Shah, Sikander Lodi and other sultans are dotted throughout the idyllic Lodi Gardens (see pp30–31). Their relatively small scale (and light style) illustrate the declining fortunes of the Sayyid and Lodi Dynasties.

6 Qutb Minar
The defining image of the Delhi Sultanate, the towering Qutb Minar (see pp24–5) is a perfect example of the simple, but grandiose, Sultanate architectural style, which was intended to symbolize both the military might of the new sultans from Afghanistan and the power of the then-newly arrived Islamic faith.

The lofty Qutb Minar

(7) Khirki Masjid

MAP V3 ■ Press Enclave Road ■ Malviya Nagar Metro ■ Open daily sunrise–sunset

Another superbly atmospheric Tughlaq-era mosque that was built in the 1370s, the Khirki Masjid looks more like a labrynthine fortress than a peaceful place of worship.

(8) Quwwat-ul-Islam

The oldest mosque in India, set in the Qutb complex *(see p24)*, this is a fascinating study in cultural contrasts. The central courtyard, fashioned out of columns from Hindu and Jain temples that previously stood on this site, has a decidedly Hindu appearance. The magnificent screen of the prayer hall, however, is a classic work of Islamic architecture covered in Koranic inscriptions.

Ornate columns at Quwwat-ul-Islam

(9) Tughlaqabad

Another monumental expression of the power of the Sultanate, the city of Tughlaqabad was built by Ghiyasuddin Tughlaq, founder of the Tughlaq Dynasty. The massive fortified citadel – now largely in ruins – was built, astonishingly, in just two years *(see p101)*.

(10) Feroz Shah Kotla

All that remains of the great city of Ferozabad *(see p88)* is a walled enclosure containing the fragmentary remains of a royal palace, mosque and other structures. The most eye-catching feature here is the Ashokan column, which is perched atop the citadel and dates from the 3rd century BC.

TOP 10 DELHI SULTANS

1 Qutbuddin Aibak
The first Delhi sultan, Qutbuddin Aibak (1150–1210) founded the Delhi Sultanate's so-called Slave Dynasty.

2 Iltutmish
The son-in-law of Aibak, Iltutmish (r. 1211–36) extended the territory of the Sultanate from Punjab to Bengal.

3 Razia Sultan
Iltutmish's daughter (r. 1236–40) and India's only major female leader until Indira Gandhi, seven centuries later.

4 Alauddin Khilji
Alauddin (r. 1296–1316) was the most illustrious ruler of the Khilji Dynasty.

5 Ghiyasuddin Tughlaq
Ghiyasuddin Tughlaq (r. 1320–24) founded the Tughlaq Dynasty.

6 Muhammad bin Tughlaq
Eccentric ruler (r. 1325–51) who tried to relocate the capital from Delhi to Daulatabad but later moved it back.

7 Feroz Shah Tughlaq
Feroz Shah Tughlaq (r. 1351–88) tried to repair the damage inflicted on the Sultanate by his predecessor.

8 Khizr Khan
Khizr Khan (r. 1414–21) took advantage of the power vacuum created by Timur's invasion in 1398 to establish the Sayyid Dynasty (1414–51).

9 Buhlul Lodi
Punjab governor (r. 1451–89) who seized power from the Sayyids, establishing the last of the Sultanate's five dynasties, the Lodi Dynasty.

10 Sikander Lodi
Sikander Lodi (r. 1489–1517) was the last effective Delhi sultan. His son, Ibrahim Lodi (r. 1517–26), was overthrown by the great Babur, the first of the Mughals.

A depiction of Razia Sultan

TOP10 Mughal Delhi Sights

Onion domes at Nizamuddin

1 Nizamuddin
The religious complex at Nizamuddin is home to several Mughal structures, including the tombs of Ataga Khan (1562) and the saint Nizamuddin Aulia (1325), both of which were built during the reign of Akbar *(see pp94–5)*.

2 Zinat ul Masjid
Dating from the reign of Aurangzeb, this neglected architectural gem is a perfect example of Mughal architecture in miniature – a scaled-down version of the Jama Masjid, with a trio of marbled onion domes sitting atop the beautifully proportioned and serene prayer hall below *(see p86)*.

3 Humayun's Tomb
Humayun's Tomb exemplifies many of the design elements that were to become standard features of the Mughal style, including the use of red sandstone with marble inlay, enormous *iwans* and the setting of the entire tomb within a very pretty Persian-style *charbagh* garden *(see pp18–19)*.

4 Purana Qila
The oldest major Mughal monument in Delhi, the walled Purana Qila was begun by Humayun and completed by his Afghan successor, Sher Shah Suri *(see p43)* after he had driven his rival into exile in Persia *(see p93)*.

5 Khan-i-Khanan
The imposing tomb of Abdur Rahim, who served as prime minister to Akbar, but later fell foul of Jahangir, is now dilapidated but still impressive. It is clearly modelled on the nearby Humayun's Tomb, though its rounded shape hints at the later Taj Mahal *(see p92)*.

6 Jama Masjid
India's largest mosque, Shah Jahan's Jama Masjid is the epitome of Mughal religious architecture: a dramatically simple combination of massive arches, domes and slender minarets, towering high above the streets of Old Delhi *(see pp16–17)*.

7 Zafar Mahal
Built by the Mughal emperor Akbar Shah II in the 18th century, and the last major monument of Mughal India, the Zafar Mahal

Humayun's Tomb

summer palace is an exercise in architectural nostalgia by an increasingly powerless, and soon to be extinguished, dynasty *(see p27)*.

8 Safdarjung's Tomb

The last major Mughal mausoleum in Delhi, Safdarjung's Tomb is generally thought to exemplify the creative decline that set in following the demise of Shah Jahan, though its fanciful façades and interior lend it a certain kitsch charm entirely its own *(see p94)*.

9 Red Fort

Despite suffering considerable damage during the 1857 Uprising and afterwards, the Red Fort remains a treasure trove of Mughal architectural styles, with imposing gateways, formal gardens and a sequence of royal pavilions strung out along the ramparts *(see pp12–13)*.

The interior of Jamali-Kamali Masjid

10 Jamali-Kamali Masjid

Completed in 1536 during Humayun's first reign *(see p19)*, the simple but elegant Jamali-Kamali Masjid is Delhi's finest example of early-Mughal architecture *(see p26)*.

TOP 10 MUGHAL DESIGN FEATURES

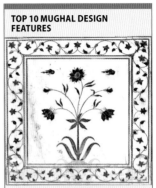

Floral pietra dura tilework

1 Red Sandstone and White Marble
A classic Mughal combination: façades of red sandstone that are decorated with bands of white marble inlay.

2 Iwans
Huge central arches providing a focus on the façades of tombs and mosques.

3 Cusped Arches
Staple of Mughal architecture, derived from Rajasthani and Bengali styles.

4 Pietra Dura
A hallmark of the Shah Jahan-era style, where colourful gemstones are embedded in white marble to create elaborate floral or abstract designs.

5 Jalis
Delicately carved marble or sandstone screens, often used to enclose tombs.

6 Tilework
A technique derived from Persia, using coloured tiles (usually, but not exclusively, blue) to decorate domes, window frames and façades.

7 Charbagh Gardens
Persian-style gardens, divided by water channels into four equal quadrants.

8 Domes
Distinctive Persian-style onion domes, often crowned with dramatic finials.

9 Chattris
Small, domed pavilions supported on four pillars, common in Hindu architecture and used on the eaves and minarets of Mughal buildings.

10 Jharokas
Distinctive balconied windows, often richly carved – another classic Hindu feature adopted by the Mughals.

🔟 Monuments of the 1857 Uprising

Muslims in the courtyard during daily prayer at Fatehpuri Masjid

1 Fatehpuri Masjid

This Chandni Chowk mosque was a hotbed of religious fervour and nationalist sentiment during the 1857 Uprising. The British responded by sacking the mosque and selling it to a local businessman, although two decades later they bought it back and returned it to Delhi's Muslim community. A number of Indian soldiers killed in the uprising lie buried in the courtyard (see p15).

2 Flagstaff Tower

MAP B4 ■ Magazine Road, Northern Ridge ■ Vidhan Sabha Metro

Built in 1828 as a British signalling post, the tower served as a shelter for dozens of civilians fleeing the city after the outbreak of hostilities during the 1857 Uprising.

The exterior of Flagstaff Tower

3 Mutiny Monument

MAP E1 ■ Rani Jhansi Road ■ Pul Bangash Metro

At the southern end of the Northern Ridge, this grandiose Gothic-style Victorian monument, built in 1863, commemorates the British soldiers (and "native" troops in British employ) killed during the uprising, with panels listing the names, ranks and numbers of military fatalities. An additional panel, added in 1972, offers an Indian perspective on the events described and is worth a look.

4 British Residency

MAP H2 ■ Sham Nath Marg ■ Kashmiri Gate Metro

The old Neo-Classical British Residency was built around the ruins of a Mughal library erected by Dara Shikoh (1615–59), son of Shah Jahan. It is now home to the Archaeology Department of the Guru Gobind Singh Indraprastha University.

5 Northern Ridge

North of Old Delhi, the northern extension of the Aravalli Range forms a long, low ridge. This is where the refugees from Delhi converged during the 1857 Uprising, and where British forces gathered before launching an assault to recapture the city (see p88).

6 St James' Church

This beautiful Colonial-era church holds a number of memorials to British civilians killed in Delhi during the 1857 Uprising. It also contains a memorial to the Reverend Midgeley John Jennings, then chaplain of Delhi, whose rather high-handed Christian evangelizing did much to enflame local religious sensibilities, and who was killed in the Red Fort during the first few hours of the revolt (see p85).

7 Magazine

MAP H2 ■ Sham Nath Marg
■ Kashmiri Gate Metro

Now marooned on a traffic island, this small British magazine was at the heart of the first day of fighting in Delhi. Surrounded by enemy Indian sepoys, the British troops stationed inside the magazine decided to blow it up rather than allow its stock of arms and ammunition to fall into Indian hands. The explosion killed around 400 sepoys and onlookers.

8 Kashmiri Gate

MAP G2 ■ Sham Nath Marg
■ Kashmiri Gate Metro

Now dwarfed by the vast new Kashmiri Gate Metro, this modest little Mughal-era gateway witnessed the most bitter fighting of the entire uprising, when British troops stormed the gate in order to force a route into the rebel-held city. A plaque at the rear commemorates those who were killed in the assault.

The Lal Darwaza or Bloody Gate

9 Lal Darwaza

MAP H6 ■ Mathura Road
■ Pragati Maidan Metro

The red sandstone Lal Darwaza (also known as the Khooni Darwaza, or Bloody Gate) marks the site of one of the most notorious episodes of the uprising, when British officer William Hodson summarily executed Mirza Mughal, Kizr Sultan and Abu Bakr, sons and grandson, respectively, of the last Mughal emperor (see p43).

10 Nicholson's Cemetery

Tucked away in Old Delhi, this atmospheric and rambling Colonial-era cemetery is a haven from the chaotic hustle and bustle of the old city. Beautifully restored in 2006, it is the final resting place of hundreds of India's early European inhabitants. Of its many graves, monuments and tombs, the most famous is that of Brigadier-General John Nicholson (1822–57), a prominent British army commander and one of the key figures in the history of the 1857 Uprising – he is best known for planning and leading the final British assault on Delhi. Nicholson was killed in September 1857 during the bitter fighting that took place for the recapture of the city (see p88).

TOP 10 Cities of Delhi, Old and New

1 Indraprastha

The legendary city of Indraprastha, home of the Pandava brothers of the epic *Mahabharata*, is said to have stood on the site that is now occupied by the Purana Qila. Conclusive evidence is sadly lacking, although finds have been unearthed here dating to the 3rd century BC, and an ancient village stood here until the early 20th century. Today this is home to one of the oldest forts in Delhi and is a great place to visit.

2 Lal Kot and Qila Rai Pithora

The first of Delhi's traditional seven cities, Lal Kot was established by a Rajput clan, the Tomars, in 1060. A century later, they became vassals of the Chauhans, who extended Lal Kot and renamed it Qila Rai Pithora. Both settlements were largely buried under the Qutb Minar complex *(see pp24-5)*.

3 Siri
MAP V2

The second city of Delhi, Siri was built during the reign of Alauddin Khilji *(see p43)*. These days little remains of it, barring a few sections of the walls. More impressive is the water tank Alauddin built nearby at Hauz Khas *(see p100)* to supply water to Siri. It was later expanded by Feroz Shah Tughlaq (r. 1351–88).

4 Tuqhlaqabad

Built during the reign of Ghiyasuddin Tughlaq (r. 1320–24), Tuqhlaqabad, the third city of Delhi, was quickly abandoned. The city's most impressive features are the massive fortified citadel and ramparts, stretching for over 6 km (4 miles), and the distinctive tomb of Ghiyasuddin himself. A smaller subsidiary fortress, known as Adilabad, stands nearby *(see p101)*.

The ancient ruined citadel and ramparts of Tuqhlaqabad

The imposing buildings of the Central Secretariat in New Delhi

 Jahanpanah

Delhi's fourth city, Jahanpanah, was built by Muhammad bin Tughlaq (see p43) shortly before the eccentric ruler briefly abandoned Delhi for the city of Daulatabad. Two important monuments survive here: the Bijay Mandal, which is thought to be Tughlaq's palace, as well as the Begumpuri Mosque (see p100).

⑥ Ferozabad

Constructed by Feroz Shah Tughlaq, Ferozabad was the fifth city of Delhi. Today, the principal surviving structure is the walled palace known as Feroz Shah Kotla (see p88), its crumbling remains topped by one of the city's two Ashokan pillars (see p88).

⑦ Purana Qila

Built on the fabled site of Indraprastha, Purana Qila – the sixth city of Delhi – was begun by the second Mughal emperor Humayun (see pp18–9) and completed by his great rival Sher Shah Suri (see p43). Following Suri's death, Humayun reclaimed the Purana Qila, but died within a year after falling down a steep flight of steps (see p93).

⑧ Shahjahanabad

Begun by Shah Jahan in 1638, Shahjahanabad (Old Delhi) was the last of Delhi's so-called seven cities. It was intended to provide North India with a capital to replace Agra.

⑨ New Delhi

Built in 1911–1931, the city of New Delhi was an attempt by the British to assert their Imperial credentials, featuring showpiece architectural landmarks including the Secretariat Buildings and the Rashtrapati Bhavan (see p21). Edwin Lutyens was asked to create a city that would rival the great cities of the Mughals and the Delhi sultans and legitimize Britain's increasingly shaky hold on the country.

⑩ Satellite Cities

Thanks to the metro, Delhi's satellite towns have become more accessible and are attracting corporations and wealthy residents. To the south, Gurugram (formerly Gurgaon) is a city of gleaming high-rises, many the headquarters of IT companies. Noida in the east, is another shiny steel-and-glass IT hub.

The satellite town of Gurugram

Museums and Galleries

① National Gallery of Modern Art (NGMA)

Located in a purpose-built structure, the National Gallery of Modern Art houses works dating from 1857 to the present. Among them are a good selection of miniatures, East India Company Art and works by classic Orientalist artists such as Thomas Daniell, as well as a collection of works by the eclectic Bengali artist Nandalal Bose *(see p80)*.

② National Museum

The National Museum is an obligatory stop on any tour of Delhi's museums. It has a superb array of exhibits covering every epoch in the country's history, ranging from priceless Harappan artifacts through to Chola bronzes and Mughal miniatures *(see pp32–5)*.

③ National Rail Museum

India's love affair with the railway is celebrated in this fine museum containing assorted antique steam engines and opulent carriages, including those once belonging to the maharajas of Mysore and Baroda, and the Prince of Wales *(see p95)*.

④ National Philatelic Museum

Heaven for stamp enthusiasts, the National Philatelic Museum holds a copy of every Indian stamp produced since Independence (around 1,700 issues), as well as an interesting selection of international stamps and the personal belongings of a mid-19th-century postman *(see p80)*.

⑤ Crafts Museum

This is another of Delhi's must-see cultural attractions, showcasing a variety of artifacts inspired by the country's indigenous folk-art traditions. Exhibits include detailed ivory carvings, as well as a vast collection of textiles and fabrics and Hindu bronzes, while outside in the grounds you can see a set of traditional buildings from all around India *(see pp28–9)*.

⑥ National Gandhi Museum

The city's second Gandhi museum is close to Raj Ghat where the body of Father of the Nation was cremated. Exhibits on display include Gandhi's memorabilia and that of his wife, plus six telephones on which visitors can listen to his famous speeches in Hindi and English *(see p88)*.

National Rail Museum

Gandhi Smriti, where Gandhi spent the last days of his life

⑦ Sulabh International Museum of Toilets

MAP A5 ■ Mahavir Enclave, Palam Dabri Marg ■ 2503 1518 ■ Uttam Nagar East Metro ■ Open 10am–5pm Mon–Sat ■ www.sulabh toiletmuseum.org

Although this museum may sound like a joke, it has quite a serious purpose, being part of the neo-Gandhian Sulabh International Movement, which aims to promote public hygiene, with many displays on lavatorial habits.

Sulabh International Museum of Toilets

⑧ Jawaharlal Nehru Memorial Museum

Teen Murti House, formerly called Flagstaff House, was built in 1930 as the residence of the British military commander-in-chief and later became home to India's first Prime Minister Jawaharlal Nehru (1889–1964). There's a library, and a few photographs and newspaper cuttings on display, but the main attraction is the house itself, including rooms left exactly as they were when Nehru lived here (see p80).

⑨ Gandhi Smriti

Formerly known as Birla House, this Neo-Classical mansion is where Gandhi (1869–1948) spent the last 144 days of his life. Displays include a touching collection of the Mahatma's personal belongings, including the watch he was wearing when he was assassinated, which stopped at the moment of his death (see p79).

⑩ Indira Gandhi Memorial Museum

This museum is the former home of Prime Minister Indira Gandhi (1917–84), who was assassinated in the garden here by two of her Sikh bodyguards. The absorbing exhibits include personal belongings and photos, plus a section devoted to her son Rajiv (1944–91), including the shoes he was wearing when he was killed by Tamil separatists in 1991 (see p78).

Exhibits at Indira Gandhi Memorial Museum

ᵀᴼᴾ10 Places of Worship

The Baha'i Temple, popularly known as the Lotus Temple

1 Baha'i Temple

India's answer to the Sydney Opera House, this remarkable building – an abstract composition inspired by the shape of an unfurling lotus flower – was built in 1986 by the Baha'is and is open to everyone. Founded by 19th-century Persian visionary Baha'u'llah, the Baha'i faith stresses the links between the major world religions and has over five million followers worldwide (see p99).

The Colonial-style St James' Church

2 St James' Church

Easily the city's most attractive church, this Colonial gem was built by the legendary Anglo-Indian soldier James Skinner (1778–1841). Barred from serving in the British army owing to his mixed race, Skinner established his own irregular cavalry regiment, Skinner's Horse, which still forms a part of the Indian army to this day (see p85).

3 Gurudwara Bangla Sahib

Built in 1783 in honour of the eighth Sikh Guru Har Krishan, this is the city's largest Sikh temple. The guru visited Delhi in 1664 during a cholera and smallpox epidemic, tending to the sick and offering them fresh water from the *sarovar* (lake) on the site, which is still believed to possess medicinal properties (see p80).

4 Zinat ul Masjid

Popularly known as the Ghata (Cloud) Masjid, this beautiful building was commissioned by Aurangzeb's daughter Zinat ul Nisa and was completed in 1707. It is the only one of the city's later Mughal monuments grand enough to rival the earlier creations of Shah Jahan (see p86).

5 Lakshmi Narayan Mandir

This eye-catching modern Hindu temple, popularly known as Birla Mandir, was commissioned by industrialist B D Birla and consecrated in 1939 by Gandhi – one of the first temples in India open to everyone, irrespective of caste. The spacious interior is centred on a shrine to Lakshmi and her consort Narayan (Vishnu), flanked by images of Durga and Shiva (see p79).

6 Nizamuddin

One of the most magical places in Delhi, the wonderfully

atmospheric religious complex of Nizamuddin grew up around the revered *dargah* (Muslim shrine) of the Chishti Sufi saint Nizamuddin Auliya. Among the cluster of structures now surrounding the saint's tomb are the Jamat Khana Masjid (1325) and the graves of the famous poet Amir Khusrau (1253–1325) and Princess Jahanara, Shah Jahan's daughter *(see p94)*.

7 Lal Mandir

This Jain temple is one of the city's most important. Topped by a cluster of towers, made of red Kota stone, it has a richly painted interior, full of diminutive marble images of various Jain gurus in glass cases. Next to the temple is a small "bird hospital", where birds are fed and cared for – evidence of the profound respect that the Jain religion has for all forms of life *(see p14)*.

Visitors at Akshardham Temple

8 Akshardham Temple

This gargantuan modern Hindu temple, inaugurated in 2005, was built in honour of the sage Bhagwan Shri Swaminarayan (1781–1830), who left his birthplace in Uttar Pradesh at the age of 11 and walked for seven years and 12,000 km (7,456 miles) before establishing an ashram in Gujarat. From here, he preached a message of non-violence and spiritual unity, attracting many Hindu followers as well as Muslim and Zoroastrian devotees *(see p94)*.

Jama Masjid, India's largest mosque

9 Begumpuri Masjid

Built in the 1340s by Muhammad bin Tughlaq as part of his city of Jahanpanah, this little-visited but atmospheric mosque is one of the finest in Delhi. The mosque is centred on a huge courtyard surrounded by domed arcades, with a fortress-like gateway leading into the prayer hall – a perfect example of Tughlaq architecture at its rugged and imposing best *(see p100)*.

10 Jama Masjid

Despite the exodus of many of the old city's Muslims during the Partition in 1947, Delhi's spectacular Jama Masjid remains a key centre for Islamic worship *(see pp16–17)*.

⓾ Parks and Gardens

Statue at Buddha Jayanti Park

1 Buddha Jayanti Park
MAP K2 ▪ Vandemataram Marg ▪ Jhandewalan Metro ▪ Open 5am–7pm daily

Hemmed in amidst the woodland of the Ridge west of New Delhi, this beautiful park was created in 1993 to mark the 2,500th anniversary of the Buddha's enlightenment. A Buddha statue sits within the park.

2 Lodi Gardens
Arguably the most attractive gardens in Delhi, with idyllic lawns and shady patches of woodland dotted with the imposing tombs of assorted Lodi and Sayyid rulers and nobles (see pp30–31).

3 Mughal Gardens
Tucked away in the grounds of Rashtrapati Bhavan, the Mughal Gardens are open to the public only for a month in spring, but are worth a visit. Designed by Edwin Lutyens in a blend of Mughal and English styles, they have many rare species of flora, including 250 varieties of rose and 60 types of bougainvillea (see p21).

4 Hauz Khas Deer Park
Close to the old tank and monuments of Hauz Khas Village (see p100), the beautiful Hauz Khas Deer Park is an area of peaceful, shady woodland, complete with pens of bounding spotted deer, roving peacocks and abundant bird life.

5 Qudsia Bagh
North of Old Delhi lies Qudsia Bagh, created in 1748 as a royal pleasure park by Qudsia Begum (1801–81), wife of Mughal emperor Muhammad Shah. Little survives of the park's original buildings apart from a florid gateway, and a delicate little mosque situated at the garden's most southeastern end (see p88).

6 Talkatora Gardens
MAP L2 ▪ Mother Teresa Crescent ▪ Open sunrise–sunset daily

Behind Rashtrapati Bhavan, these 18th-century gardens are among central Delhi's most popular parks. They are prettiest in spring when the colourful shrubs burst into life.

7 Garden of Five Senses
MAP V3 ▪ Said-ul-Ajaib village, near Mahavirsthal on the Mehrauli–Badarpur Road ▪ Saket Metro ▪ Open 8am–9pm daily ▪ Adm

This is Delhi's most artistic garden, dotted with sculptures. The gardens themselves are divided into differently landscaped areas, with sensory themes and names such as the "Trail of Fragrance" and "Colour Gardens".

8 Nehru Park
MAP L6 ■ Panchsheel Road, Chanyakapuri ■ Open 5am–8pm daily

Covering almost 32 ha (80 acres), Nehru Park is one of the most popular retreats in South Delhi, with spacious lawns and a pool. The park frequently hosts concerts.

9 Raj Ghat
These gardens are best known as the place where the funeral rites of modern India's most important leaders took place, including Mahatma Gandhi, Indira Gandhi, Rajiv Gandhi and Jawaharlal Nehru, each of whom is commemorated with a monument (see p85).

Mahatma Gandhi memorial, Raj Ghat

10 Coronation Park
MAP B4 ■ Shanti Swaroop Tyagi Marg, near Nirankari Sarovar ■ Open sunrise–sunset daily

Some 19 km (12 miles) north of Connaught Place, this was the site of the three British Durbars of 1887, 1903 and 1911. After independence, the park was used as a dumping ground for Raj-era statues, including a statue of King George V that once stood in front of India Gate.

Mughal Gardens

TOP 10 INDIAN TREES

The flowers of the gulmohar tree

1 Champa (*Plumeria rubra*)
A species of frangipani, this is one of the most common Indian flowering shrubs, producing huge white blooms.

2 Neeli Gulmohar (*Jacaranda mimosifolia*)
The jacaranda is a flowering tree, which explodes in spring into a very distinctive purple-blue blossom.

3 Peepul (*Ficus religiosa*)
A species of banyan fig, this is also Buddhism's sacred tree (commonly known as the bodhi tree).

4 Amaltas (*Cassia fistula*)
A shrub (Indian laburnum in English) with Ayurvedic properties, this bursts into cascading yellow flowers in spring.

5 Gulmohar (*Delonix regia*)
The Indian flame tree has distinctive fern-like leaves and bright red flowers.

6 Semal (*Bombax ceiba*)
The red silk cotton tree is an attractive ornamental tree and especially pretty in spring, when it is covered in vibrant red flowers, with no leaves.

7 Jamun (*Syzygium cumini*)
The evergreen black plum is known for its large purple berries. It also features in the epic, the *Ramayana*.

8 Kachnar (*Bauhinia variegata*)
The popular ornamental orchid tree has scented pink or white flowers.

9 Dhak (*Butea monosperma*)
This pretty flowering species, known as the flame of the forest in English, has curved, bright orange flowers.

10 Neem (*Azadirachta indica*)
A common South Asian tree (Indian lilac), the neem is renowned for its medicinal properties, hence its popular description as the "village pharmacy".

TOP 10 Delhi-Inspired Books

Indian author Anita Desai

Hardy as a reporter for *The Indian Express*, offers fascinating insights into the city's complex social fabric, from the lives of local slum dwellers to the Westernized airs of Delhi's high-flying aristocratic elite.

(4) Trees of Delhi: A Field Guide (Pradip Krishen)

With a total ban on high-rise constructions still effective across large parts of the capital, Delhi's skyline is dominated not just by buildings but by trees. Ecologist and tree-lover Pradip Krishen's field guide provides an excellent introduction to some of the common varieties of trees that dot the city which, by many accounts, has become greener over recent years.

(5) The Delhi Omnibus (introduction by Narayani Gupta)

The omnibus captures not just the physical history of the city, but the manner in which the people have invented and reinvented themselves over time. It contains writings by Percival Spear, Narayani Gupta, R E Frykenberg and Christopher Bayly.

(1) Clear Light of Day (Anita Desai)

This is Anita Desai's most obviously autobiographical work, centred on the contrasting stories of two sisters from Old Delhi – one of whom leaves the city and the other of whom remains – and their subsequent reunion.

(2) The White Tiger (Aravind Adiga)

A Booker Prize-winning debut novel by Chennai-born Aravind Adiga, this is partly set in Delhi, and relates the murderous career of anti-hero Balram Halwai, with insights into contemporary Indian society en route.

(3) Scoop-wallah: Life On a Delhi Daily (Justine Hardy)

This engrossing account of a year spent by English journalist Justine

Delhi: Adventures in a Megacity

(6) Delhi: Adventures in a Megacity (Sam Miller)

This very entertaining eye-witness account of contemporary Delhi follows a spiralling perambulation through the city, from the centre of Connaught Place out into the suburbs, with wonderfully evocative descriptions of the many people and places encountered on the journey.

(7) Delhi: A Novel (Khushwant Singh)

This is an engaging novel by one of India's foremost modern writers.

Historical snapshots of the city through the ages – culminating in the anti-Sikh riots of 1984 – are interspersed with a secondary narrative about a journalist and the passionate relationship he develops with a *hijra* (eunuch).

8 City of Djinns (William Dalrymple)

A beautifully written portrait of Delhi's multilayered personality, this book is particularly strong on the city's history, interspersed with richly comic snapshots of the modern city.

9 Twilight in Delhi (Ahmed Ali)

A novel by Delhi-born Ahmed Ali, this paints a beautiful portrait of the city at the beginning of the 20th century – an elegiac lament for the city's rapidly disappearing Mughal traditions in the face of the Colonial and European cultural onslaught.

10 The Last Mughal (William Dalrymple)

A landmark study of the 1857 Uprising, drawing on unpublished contemporary source. This is the most even-handed account of the conflict yet published in English.

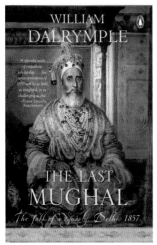

The Last Mughal (William Dalrymple)

TOP 10 DELHI FILMS

Monsoon Wedding (2001)

1 Fire (1996)
A controversial tale of a lesbian affair between two Delhi housewives.

2 Monsoon Wedding (2001)
Mira Nair's marvellously evocative portrait of the people and places of contemporary Delhi, combining social comedy with stunning cinematography.

3 Rang De Basanti (2006)
An influential film by director Rakeysh Omprakash Mehra about five young men who are trying to expose India's widespread political corruption.

4 Khosla Ka Ghosla! (2006)
A comedy drama depicting the battle between a middle-class family and a real-estate shark over a plot of land.

5 Oye Lucky! Lucky Oye! (2008)
A comedy with Abhay Deol playing a "super thief" alongside a lovable host of rather disreputable characters.

6 Delhi-6 (2009)
A Rakeysh Omprakash Mehra film depicting the lives and loves of an eclectic array of Old Delhi characters.

7 Dev.D (2009)
Clever, contemporary reworking of the classic Bengali movie *Devdas*.

8 Vicky Donor (2012)
Reflecting a city coming to grips with modernity, with Ayushmann Khurrana as a Punjabi sperm donor who falls in love with a wordly Bengali banker.

9 Band Baajaa Baraat (2010)
A refreshing love story following the ups and downs of two rival wedding planners in modern Delhi.

10 Delhi Belly (2011)
A black comedy, starring Imran Khan, about three friends who share a room in Delhi and somehow get involved in an underworld crime plot.

🔟 Off the Beaten Track

1 Shankar's International Dolls Museum

MAP H6 ▪ 4 Bahadur Shah Zafar Marg ▪ 2331 6970 ▪ Open 10am–6pm Tue–Sun (last entry 5:30pm) ▪ Adm ▪ www.childrensbooktrust.com/dollsmuseum.html

Doll enthusiasts will love this prodigious collection of over 6,000 dolls from around the world, many dressed in regional and national costumes, and including amusing mannequins of John Wayne, Louis Armstrong and Henry VIII.

2 Majnu ka Tila

MAP B4 ▪ Aruna Nagar, Outer Ring Road ▪ 15 min walk or short auto-rickshaw ride from Vidhan Sabha Metro

Here in Delhi's little Tibet the Dalai Lama's image beams down from the wall of almost every establishment. Visitors can purchase prayer wheels, *thangkas* (traditional Buddhist religious paintings), books about Tibet and excellent Tibetan food.

Prayer wheels, Majnu ka Tila

3 Adhchini

MAP V2 ▪ Qutab Enclave, Aurobindo Marg ▪ Hauz Khas Metro

An urban village, with residents, who mainly belong to an ethnic group called the Jats, Adhchini contains a 16th-century Lodi mosque and an impressive shrine to the mother of Nizamuddin Auliya (see p94).

4 Kalan Masjid

MAP G5 ▪ In an alley opposite 2063 Mohammed Deen Haichi Marg

Built in 1387 and older than Old Delhi itself, this blue-and-green mosque, located near Turkman Gate, was – along with Khirki Masjid (see p45) – one of seven mosques commissioned by Feroz Shah's chief minister Khan-i-Jahan Junan Shah. It is the only one still in use today.

5 Masjid Mubarak Begum

MAP G4 ▪ 4959 Hauz Razi, Lalkuan Bazaar Road ▪ Chawri Bazaar Metro

This charming little private mosque was built in 1823 for the Indian wife of Sir David Ochterlony, British Resident at the Mughal Court. Hidden away above a busy bazaar, and accessed by a narrow stairway between two shops (guests must take their shoes off at the top), it has a tiny prayer hall with only enough room for ten worshippers.

6 Surajkund Dam
Anangpur, 20 km (12 miles)
S of central Delhi, 4 km (2 miles)
W of NHPC Chowk metro station
■ Surajkund Tank: open sunrise–
sunset daily ■ Adm

Way off the beaten track, but still within easy reach of the metro, this is Delhi's very oldest construction, built under the Tomar king Anangpal in the 8th century to store rainwater for irrigation. Surajkund Tank, 2 km (1 mile) to its north, is an ancient 10th-century reservoir, which was also built under the Tomars.

7 Aliganj
MAP N7 ■ Between Aliganj Road and Karbala Road, Jor Bagh ■ Jor Bagh Metro ■ shahemardan.org

Once the estate of the Shiite rulers of Awadh, the family of the Nawab of Safdarjung, this neighbourhood has some interesting 18th-century buildings, most notably the Shah-e-Mardan Dargah, a Shia shrine where Sunnis and Hindus also sometimes go to pray.

8 Chhattarpur Mandir
MAP B7 ■ Main Chhattarpur Road ■ 2680 2925 ■ Chhattarpur Metro ■ Open 6am–10pm daily ■ www.chhattarpurmandir.org

This was the biggest temple in India when it was built in 1974, but it is really a park-like compound with several temples inside it, presided over by a 30-m (98-ft) high statue of the monkey god, Hanuman. The complex was financed by followers of a guru known as Babaji, whose ashes rest in one of the temples.

Paharganj Christian Cemetery

9 Paharganj Christian Cemetery
MAP E5 ■ Ramdwara Road, Nehru Bazaar ■ 2358 5710 ■ Open daily

It is easy to forget that Christianity is an important religion in India, where three states still have Christian majorities. This little cemetery has faithfully served Delhi's Christian community since the 19th century, but really comes to life on Halloween, when it sparkles with candles left by relatives visiting the deceased.

10 Bijay Mandal
MAP V2 ■ Kalu Sarai, near Hauz Khas Metro

Around 100 m (330 ft) north of Begumpuri Masjid (see p100), this sturdy but atmospheric ruin is all that remains of sultan Muhammad bin Tughlaq's palace. Visitors can climb to the octagonal pavilion on its roof for great views over the city.

The Chhattarpur Mandir complex

🔟 Performing Arts Venues

Classical dance performance during a show at Kamani Auditorium

1 Kamani Auditorium
MAP Q1 ■ Mandi House,
1 Copernicus Marg ■ 4350 3351
■ Mandi House Metro ■ www.
kamaniauditorium.org

The Kamani Auditorium is one of the city's leading venues for classical music and dance, attracting leading performers from across the country.

2 Triveni Kala Sangam
MAP G7 ■ 205 Tansen
Marg ■ 2371 8833 ■ Mandi
House Metro

This cultural centre houses a range of venues, including galleries, an auditorium and an open-air theatre, which stages regular music and dance performances.

3 Shri Ram Centre for Performing Arts
MAP Q1 ■ 4 Safdar Hashmi
Marg ■ 2371 4307
■ Mandi House Metro
■ www.shriramcentre.org

Established in 1975, this is an important theatrical venue, with its own outstanding repertory company, staging a wide range of interesting productions that include musical, traditional and experimental theatre.

4 Sangeet Natak Akademi
MAP P1 ■ Rabindra Bhavan,
35 Feroz Shah Road ■ 2338 7246
■ Mandi House Metro ■ www.
sangeetnatak.org

This is one of the country's foremost performing arts venues, and home to Delhi's finest open-air theatre. It also has a library and a gallery featuring a range of traditional musical instruments, masks and puppets.

5 National School of Drama
MAP Q1 ■ Bahawalpur
House, 1 Bhagwan Das Road
■ 2338 2821 ■ Mandi House
Metro ■ www.nsd.gov.in

The National School of Drama (NSD) is the country's leading academy for aspiring actors. The productions are staged by current students and the school's professional repertory company.

National School of Drama

6 Parsi Anjuman Hall
MAP H5 ■ Bahadur Shah
Zafar Marg ■ 2323 8615 ■ Pragati
Maidan Metro

Home to the Dances of India show (daily at 6:45pm), featuring a programme of classical and folk dances.

7 India International Centre

MAP P6 ■ 40 Max Mueller Marg ■ 2461 9431 ■ www.iicdelhi.nic.in

Besides regular music, dance and theatrical performances, the India International Centre (IIC) hosts exhibitions and talks attracting leading cultural personalities from Salman Rushdie to Noam Chomsky. It also hosts a popular cinema club with art-house film screenings.

8 Nizamuddin

The fascinating religious enclave of Nizamuddin is Delhi's most atmospheric venue for impromptu music, with nightly performances of ecstatic *qawwali* singing around the shrine of Nizamuddin Auliya, the famous Sufi saint (see p94).

9 Siri Fort

MAP V2 ■ Khel Gaon Marg ■ 2649 3370 ■ Green Park Metro

The extensive Siri Fort Cultural Complex boasts three auditoriums (the largest seating almost 2,000 people), staging a range of big-name events, particularly Indian classical music concerts, dance and film.

10 India Habitat Centre

MAP P6 ■ Lodi Road ■ 2468 2001 ■ www.indiahabitat.org

This is one of Delhi's state-of-the-art performing-arts venues, and hosts regular music, dance and cultural events such as art-house film screenings and talks.

Bhangra at the India Habitat Centre

TOP 10 FORMS OF INDIAN CLASSICAL MUSIC

A group of *qawwali* singers

1 Raga and Khayal
The system of modes underlying all Indian classical music, a framework for composition and improvisation. A *khayal* is the extended, improvised elaboration of a raga using a lyrical composition called a *bandish*.

2 Dhrupad
One of the oldest and most austere forms of Hindustani classical vocal music, said to have developed from the chanting of Vedic hymns.

3 Thumri
A type of love song, usually performed in Braj Bhasha, a dialect of Hindi.

4 Dadra
A light form of Hindustani classical vocal music popular in north India.

5 Tarana
North Indian vocal genre involving the rapid singing of musical syllables based on Persian/Arabic phonemes.

6 Kriti
The major vocal genre of Carnatic music, divided into three parts, and with a religious theme.

7 Varnam
Form of Carnatic vocal music designed to bring out the qualities of the underlying raga.

8 Padam
Light classical love songs in the Carnatic tradition, often sung during Bharatanatyam dance performances.

9 Ghazal
Persian-derived light classical song form, often using lyrics by Urdu poets.

10 Qawwali
Sufi devotional music, with ecstatic, rhythmic singing used by devotees to achieve the trance-like state that Sufis believe brings them closer to God.

Places to Eat

1 Olive Bar & Kitchen

Located in the rustic yet swanky One Style Mile, Olive Bar & Kitchen is one of the prettiest restaurants in town, with a lovely, airy courtyard and the Qutb Minar providing a stunning backdrop. The food here, mainly Indian, Italian and Mediterranean, is delicious too *(see p105)*.

Indian Accent fusion cuisine

2 SodaBottleOpenerWala

Straight out of Bombay but with a strong Iranian influence, this restaurant specializes in the food of the Parsi community. As well as *dhansak*, there are more adventurous dishes such as sweet-and-sour *brinjal patio* or the berry *pulao*, made famous by Bombay's Britannia restaurant *(see p97)*. Baked goodies include ginger biscuit and *mawa cake*.

3 Chor Bizarre

This place specializes in excellent Kashmiri dishes rarely found elsewhere, such as *goshtaba* (slow-cooked mutton in yoghurt and cardamon) and a wonderful Kashmiri version of *dum aloo (see p89)*. The decor is delightfully eccentric.

4 Indian Accent

A superb modern Indian fusion restaurant, where the dishes run to paneer tikka quesadillas, tofu coriander vadas and tandoori bacon prawns. It can be difficult to make a decision with a range of innovative local dishes so it's worth checking the excellent vegetarian and non-vegetarian tasting menus on offer *(see p104)*.

5 Saravana Bhavan

An excellent and inexpensive south Indian vegetarian restaurant, where diners can feast on *idli sambar*, *masala dosa* and many other south Indian specialities, or tuck into a tasty vegetarian *thali*. If that is too filling, visitors can go for the mini tiffin, which offers a small taste of everything on the menu *(see p83)*.

6 Spice Route

This elegant hotel restaurant offers guests a special dining experience. The cuisine is from southeast Asia and the Indian state of Kerala – it is fiery, and the emphasis is on fish and seafood. A tasting menu is available in the evenings *(see p83)*.

Diners at Chor Bizarre, with its whimsical decor

7 Wasabi By Morimoto

Dark wood sets the tone for this top-class Japanese restaurant. After a drink at the exclusive sake bar, sample some steamed oysters followed by tenderloin *teppenyaki*. Round the meal off with a pungent, yet surprisingly cooling, serving of wasabi sorbet (see p83).

Table setting at Bukhara

8 Bukhara

With a guest list that includes former US President Bill Clinton, Bukhara offers a rich menu that includes the city's best-loved dishes. The buttery *dal bukhara* (lentils) is legendary, as is the succulent, melt-in-the-mouth lamb dish and the *Sikandari raan* (see p97).

9 The China Kitchen

A far cry from the usual Indian-influenced Chinese fare served up in the city, the food in The China Kitchen is modern and experimental yet still deeply rooted in traditional, primarily Szechuan, flavours. Diners swear the Peking Duck is the best in Delhi (see p105).

10 Karim's

Boasting a line of chefs that, apparently, used to prepare meals for Mughal emperors, Karim's is arguably the city's most famous restaurant. Try the excellent mutton *korma* and *seekh kebabs* (see p89).

TOP 10 BARS AND NIGHTCLUBS

1 PCO
A "speakeasy" boasting retro decor, a well-stocked bar and exotic cocktails. Requires a secret code – periodically changed – for entry (see p103).

2 Aqua
An elegant spot for drinks, with an iridescent pool, curtained pavilions and designer bar (see p82).

3 1911
A quiet, elegant Art Deco place that is steeped in old-world charm (see p82).

4 OTW (On the Waterfront)
An elegant bar at the Lodhi serving the best wine in town (see p97).

5 Club Pangaea
MAP L6 ▪ The Ashok Hotel, 50-B Diplomatic Enclave, Chanakyapuri ▪ 3014 6033 ▪ Open 7pm–1am daily
An exclusive nightclub serving some of the city's best malts and wines.

6 Baci
A refined option ideal for an early evening tête-à-tête, but transforms into a party hot-spot at the weekend. Very popular with the city's expatriate crowd. Generous cocktails (see p97).

7 Fio Cookhouse & Bar
Great thin-crust pizzas and potent cocktails with a twist (see p105).

8 G-Bar
MAP T2 ▪ The Grand, Nelson Mandela Marg ▪ 2677 1234 ▪ Open 6pm–3am daily
Attracts a young crowd with its lively music and upbeat atmosphere.

9 Kylin
An atmospheric bar with excellent cocktails and fruity sangria (see p103).

10 Kitty Su
Colourful nightclub off Connaught Place with a vibrant atmosphere and regular concerts and events (see p82).

The elegant, alfresco Aqua

Bazaars of Old Delhi

1 Dariba Kalan
MAP H3 ■ Chandni Chowk
■ Chandni Chowk Metro ■ Open
11am–8pm Mon–Sat

Dating back to the days of Emperor Shah Jahan, "The Street of the Incomparable Pearl" is Old Delhi's foremost jewellery bazaar. The shops here sell an array of precious stones and metals including an especially good selection of silverware, as well as traditional attar-based *itr* perfumes.

2 Ballimaran
MAP G3 ■ Chandni Chowk
■ Chandni Chowk Metro ■ Open
11am–8pm Mon–Sat

The Chandni Chowk end of this long Old Delhi thoroughfare is the place to go to for shoes and slippers.

Dry fruits on sale at Khari Baoli

3 Khari Baoli
MAP F3 ■ Chandni Chowk
■ Chandni Chowk Metro ■ Open
11am–8pm Mon–Sat

Said to be the biggest spice market in Asia, Khari Baoli is one of Old Delhi's most absorbing sights. Lively and congested in equal measure, it is

The crowded stalls of Kinari Bazaar

lined with shops crammed full of all kinds of spices, pulses, dried fruits and other cooking ingredients.

4 Kinari Bazaar
MAP G3 ■ Chandni Chowk
■ Chandni Chowk Metro ■ Open
11am–8pm Mon–Sat

Just off Dariba Kalan, the shops of Kinari Bazaar are famous for their wedding paraphernalia and other "fancy goods" – garlands of fake flowers and banknotes, reams of gold and silver tinsel, bridal veils, turbans for grooms and sparkly costume jewellery. They also sell items used in the *Ramayana* performances that are staged all over the city during the festival of Dussehra.

5 Guliyan Bazaar
MAP G4 ■ Chawri Bazaar Metro

Stretching around the northwestern side of Jama Masjid, this is the place to come to stock up on fireworks for a wedding or a festival, with shops filled with piles of brightly coloured boxes full of rockets, firecrackers and other things that go bang.

6 Nai Sarak
MAP G4 ■ Chawri Bazaar Metro

This street, created by the British in 1857 (hence the name, meaning "New Street"), cuts across the heart of the old city. It is now Old Delhi's main book market, with small shops selling dog-eared, second-hand school and college textbooks.

(7) Car Parts Bazaar
MAP G4 ■ Chawri Bazaar Metro

Sprawling around the south and west sides of the Jama Masjid, this is one of Old Delhi's more workaday bazaars selling mechanical bits and bobs. Visitors will find everything from wheels, doors, hubcaps, panels and entire engines – a surreal sight in the shadow of the beautiful mosque.

(8) Katra Neel
MAP G3 ■ Chandni Chowk ■ Chandni Chowk Metro ■ Open 11am–8pm Mon–Sat

Just off Chandni Chowk, this fascinating labyrinth of tiny alleyways is cluttered with shops selling all manner of ladies' clothing – shawls, salwar kameezes, saris – and a wide variety of textiles, such as brocades from Benarasi, silk and voile.

(9) Chawri Bazaar
MAP G4 ■ Chawri Bazaar Metro

Old Delhi's stationery bazaar is devoted to writing paper, greetings cards and other paper products. Paper here is sold by weight and is very cheap. Shops at the western end of the road specialize in lovely brass and copper ornaments.

(10) Meena Bazaar
MAP H4 ■ Chawri Bazaar Metro

On the steps around the Jama Masjid is Old Delhi's religious bazaar, with stalls selling prayer rugs, Koranic inscriptions, pictures of Mecca and Islamic-style clocks *(see p16)*.

A shoe stall at Meena Bazaar

TOP 10 SHOPS AND MARKETS

Colourful handicrafts at Dilli Haat

1 Daryaganj Sunday Book Market
MAP H5 ■ Open 7am–7pm Sun
A huge Sunday market for inexpensive second-hand books, most in English, fiction and non-fiction alike.

2 State Emporia Complex
MAP F7 ■ A–5 Baba Kharak Singh Marg
A must-visit for anyone interested in India's rich arts and crafts heritage.

3 Janpath Market
MAP F7 ■ Janpath ■ Open daily
Everything from export-reject clothes to pretty handmade paper lanterns.

4 Khan Market
MAP P5 ■ Open 10am–7:30pm Mon–Sat
Chic shops and restaurants, plus smaller shops selling lovely trinkets.

5 Santushti
ITC Maurya, Sardar Patel Marg ■ Open 10am–7pm Mon–Sat
Classy shopping complex selling an assortment of beautiful designerwear.

6 Connaught Place
Elegant Georgian-style crescents housing Delhi's most important commercial space *(see p77)*.

7 Hauz Khas Village
MAP U2 ■ Hauz Khas Village ■ Open 10am–8:30pm Mon–Sat
Lovely art galleries, cafés and shops.

8 Sarojini Nagar
MAP V1 ■ Sarojini Nagar ■ Open 10am–8:30pm Tue–Sun
Cheap heaps of export-reject clothes.

9 Dilli Haat
A range of Indian craft items *(see p96)*.

10 Select Citywalk Complex
MAP V3 ■ A-3 District Centre Saket ■ 4211 4211 ■ Open 10am–11pm daily
Luxurious mall with stores offering major international brand names.

Delhi for Free

The fascinating ruins at Mehrauli Archaeological Park

1 Mehrauli Archaeological Park

With over 70 monuments, including tombs, mosques, gateways and stepwells, from every century between the 13th and the 19th, this extensive park is full of interesting sights and is also free to visit (see p100).

2 Films and Concerts

Alliance Française: 72 K K Birla Marg, Lodi Estate; delhi.afindia.org ■ American Center: 24 Kasturba Gandhi Marg; in.usembassy.gov.
Cultural centres such as the American Center and the Alliance Française often host free movies, concerts and other events, although visitors may have to register or get passes in advance. The National Gandhi Museum (see p52) puts on free films about Gandhi's life (in English on Saturdays at 4pm).

3 Museums for Free

All open Tue–Sun, mostly 10am–5pm
Not far from one another, Gandhi Smriti (see p79), the Indira Gandhi Memorial Museum (see p78) and the Jawaharlal Nehru Memorial Museum (see p80) are all free, as are, at the other end of New Delhi, the National Gallery of Modern Art (see p80) and the Crafts Museum (see pp28–9). The National Gandhi Museum (see p52), the National Philatelic Museum (see p52) and the Sulabh International Museum of Toilets (see p53) are also free.

4 Open-Air Gyms

Lodi Gardens, Nehru Park and other locations ■ Park opening hours
Those looking for a free outdoor workout are in luck. The New Delhi Municipal Council has installed an array of fitness equipment in the Lodi Gardens (see pp30–31) and Nehru Park (see p57), and now plans to roll them out in parks across the city.

5 Changing of the Guard

MAP L3 ■ Gate No. 2 Rashtrapati Bhavan, Rajpath ■ 15 Mar–14 Aug: 8am Sat (except in bad weather); 15 Aug–14 Nov: 9am Sat; 15 Nov–14 Mar: 10am Sat ■ www.presidentof india.nic.in/changing-of-the-guard.htm
Although visits to see the interior of the presidential palace (see pp20–21) incur a small booking fee, the weekly Changing of the Guard ceremony is free; just bring your passport.

Flag bearers at the Changing of the Gua

6. Hindu temples

Mostly daily, dawn to late evening, but some have shorter opening hours

All Hindu temples are free to enter as long as you dress respectfully. The most popular are three modern temples – Akshardham Temple (see p94), Chhattarpur Mandir (see p61) and Lakshmi Narayan Mandir (see p79) – and the Gauri Shankar Mandir in Old Delhi (see p88).

7. Hauz Khas

MAP U2 ■ Hauz Khas Village Road

Alauddin Khilji's 14th-century Hauz-i-Alai reservoir (see p100) is free to visit, as is the nearby Deer Park (see p56). The road into the village from Aurobindo Marg has a string of 14th- and 15th-century tombs along it; these are also free to everyone.

8. Jahanpanah

MAP V–W2 ■ Between the Outer Ring Road, Press Enclave Marg, Aurobindo Marg and Lal Bahadur Shastri Marg

Delhi's fourth incarnation (see p51) is full of fascinating free sights, from the Begumpuri Masjid (see p100) and Bijay Mandal (see p61) to the Khirki Masjid (see p45) and Chiragh Delhi village (p101). Combined, they add up to a wonderful half-day walk.

9. Qawwalis in Nizamuddin

MAP R6 ■ Hazrat Nizamuddin Dargah, Nizamuddin ■ 98117 78607 ■ Open 5:30–7pm & 7:45–9pm daily ■ www.nizamuddinaulia.org

Anyone can attend Nizamuddin's dargah (see p94) to hear qawwalis, the rhythmic chanting and singing used by devotees to achieve a trance-like state. Visitors should dress respectfully, as this is a religious shrine.

10. Gurudwara Bangla Sahib

Delhi's biggest Sikh temple offers free guided tours on request, with devotional music on tap, and a free meal of dal and chapattis three times daily for everyone (see p54).

TOP 10 BUDGET TIPS

Auto-rickshaws in Old Delhi

1 The metro is much cheaper than a taxi or auto-rickshaw, and usually faster, with no haggling.

2 For auto-rickshaws, use the pre-paid booths at Connaught Place, Janpath and transport terminals, paying an official set rate to avoid overcharging.

3 Don't buy holiday reading before your trip: bookshops in Delhi stock the latest bestsellers, for less than half the price that many would pay at home.

4 Most bars in Delhi have a happy hour early in the evening, typically with "buy one get one free" offers on Indian beers and spirits.

5 A coffee at the India Coffee House (see p82) costs about a quarter of the price charged by other espresso chains.

6 Alternatively, drink tea: a nice, warming cup of pukka chai will cost around ten rupees on any street corner.

7 Have a meal at a dhaba (local diner). If the food is freshly cooked, then hygiene shouldn't be an issue. If the menu isn't in English, it's a good idea to confirm the price before ordering.

8 It is possible to get a bespoke suit made by a tailor at Connaught Place, such as M Ram and Sons (see p81). Needless to say, it will cost a fraction of the price charged back home.

9 A ticket for the Taj Mahal gives travellers a discounted rate for entry to Fatehpur Sikri and several sites around Agra if they go on the same day.

10 One or two of Delhi's best restaurants offer slightly less expensive set menus. At Bukhara (see p65), there's a lunchtime set menu, while Spice Route (see p64), by contrast, has a tasting menu in the evening.

🔟 Festivals and Events

A marching regiment at the Indian Republic Day Parade

1 Republic Day Parade
26 Jan

India's biggest parade celebrates the inauguration of the Indian constitution on 26 January 1950. The parade begins at the foot of Raisina Hill (see p20) and ends at the Red Fort, with military march pasts, floats and a fly-past by the Indian Air Force.

2 Beating the Retreat
29 Jan

Signalling the official end of the Republic Day celebrations, this ceremony recalls the old battlefield tradition of soldiers halting hostilities at the end of the day. It is held at Vijay Chowk (see p21) and features a parade of soldiers accompanied by military bands.

3 Surajkund Crafts Mela
A fortnight in Feb

Held in Surajkund, about 20 km (12 miles) south of Delhi, this is one of India's biggest craft fairs, showcasing works from all over the country, with musicians and dancers creating a lively carnival-esque atmosphere.

Surajkund Crafts Mela handicrafts

4 Vintage Car Rally
Late Feb/Early Mar

This car rally features around 100 vintage and postwar cars, with their owners dressed in period costume. The event starts and ends in central Delhi and attracts participants from all over the country.

5 National School of Drama Festivals
May and Jun ▪ Adm

Each year, the National School of Drama (see p62) hosts the Summer Theatre Festival, with a variety of classical and contemporary plays staged by the school's professional repertory company. In spring, it hosts the Bharat Rang Mahotsav, with plays by theatre companies from across the world.

6 International Mango Festival
Late Jun/Early Jul

Mango lovers can sample more than 500 different types of mango that are on offer at this annual celebration of the delicious yellow fruit. The event is held at held at Talkatora Gardens (see p56) every year.

(7) Phool Walon ki Sair
Usually 3 days in Sep

The colourful Festival of the Flower Sellers is held in Mehrauli *(see p100)* after the rainy season. The highlight is the procession of flower sellers, who carry ornate floral tributes to the shrine of Qutb Sahib *(see p26)*. They are led by dancers and people playing the *shehnai*, a type of woodwind instrument whose sound is thought to create a sense of sanctity.

(8) Old Fort Dance Festival
Early Oct

A free, five-day festival of classical Indian dance at the medieval Purana Qila fort *(see p93)*. Visitors experience the very best of Indian dance, from the graceful storytelling Kathak of northern India to Kerala's mesmerizing Mohiniyattam and Tamil Nadu's spiritual Bharatanatyam.

Performers at the Purana Qila fort

(9) The IIC Experience
Mid-Oct

Held at the IIC *(see p63)*, this festival of the arts hosts a wide range of cultural events from music and dance (both Indian and Western) to theatre, film and literature, and is accompanied by a good food festival.

(10) Qutb Festival
Nov/Dec

A three-day music festival, with concerts held in the Qutb Minar Complex *(see pp24–5)*, ranging from soulful *qawwali* singers and virtuoso sitar players to young rock bands.

TOP 10 RELIGIOUS FESTIVALS

A devotee with an idol of Ganesh

1 Maha Shivaratri
The "Great Night of Shiva", marked with fasts and prayers (late Feb/early Mar).

2 Holi
Indian spring festival, with bonfires lit the day before and people dousing each other with coloured powder and water on the day (usually Mar).

3 Rama Navami
Celebration of the birth of Rama, with continuous readings of the epic *Ramayana*, accompanied by singing and prayers (late Mar/early Apr).

4 Buddha Jayanti
Celebration of the Buddha's birth, enlightenment and death (May).

5 Krishna Janmashtami
One-day festival celebrating the birth of Lord Krishna (mid-Aug–mid-Sep).

6 Ganesh Chaturthi
Ten-day festival celebrating the birth of Lord Ganesh with colourful processions (mid-Aug–mid-Sep).

7 Dussehra
Ten-day festival celebrating the victory of good over evil, including Rama's victory over Ravana and Durga's defeat of Mahishasura (mid-Sep–mid-Oct).

8 Bakr Id
The year's biggest Muslim festival, when the Jama Masjid area becomes a market for sacrificial goats (Sep/Oct).

9 Diwali
Five-day festival of lights in honour of Lord Rama's return to Ayodhya from exile, marked with the lighting of lamps and fireworks (Oct/Nov).

10 Guru Purab
A series of ten Sikh festivals, each celebrating the birth of one of the Sikh faith's ten gurus (through the year).

Excursions from Delhi

A monkey outside Mathura temple

③ Deeg
MAP B3 ■ Deeg Palace: Open 8am–5pm daily ■ Adm

This workaday town is home to one of the region's most spectacular palaces. Built in the 18th century by the local Jat rulers, the Deeg Palace blends Hindu and Mughal elements with spacious water gardens dotted with palaces and pavilions. The celebrated Keshav Bhawan (known as Monsoon Palace) was designed to re-create the torrential rainfall and thunderous sounds of a wet-season downpour.

① Mathura and Vrindavan
MAP C3

Mathura is reputed to be the birth place of the flute-playing deity, Krishna, while half a million pilgrims a year flock to the nearby town of Vrindavan and the hill of Govardhan, which Krishna is said to have lifted with just a single finger.

② Amritsar
MAP B1

The holiest city of the Sikh faith is home to the Golden Temple, an unforgettable sight with the gilded Harmandir Sahib rising out of the surrounding lake.

④ Sultanpur Bird Sanctuary
MAP B3 ■ 45 km (28 miles) SW of Delhi ■ Open 6am–4:30pm Wed–Mon ■ Adm and charge for video

Around 45 km (28 miles) southwest of Delhi in Haryana state, the Sultanpur Bird Sanctuary makes for a peaceful rural outing. Centred on a large wetland area that fills up during the seasonal rains, the sanctuary attracts aquatic migratory birds and offers a number of walks through the surrounding woods.

Sultanpur Bird Sanctuary

⑤ Keoladeo Ghana National Park
MAP C3 ■ Bharatpur district, 185 km (115 miles) E of Jaipur ■ Open Apr–Sep: 6am–6pm; Oct–Mar: 6:30am–5:30pm ■ Adm

This wonderful national park near the town of Bharatpur is arguably India's finest birdwatching destination. It is home to a huge number of resident and migratory species, including flocks of aquatic birds who come to nest in the park's wetlands.

⑥ Sariska Tiger Reserve

MAP B3 ▪ Alwar district, 37 km (23 miles) SW of Alwar ▪ 78383 48955 ▪ Open 6am–4pm daily (call in advance to check for timings)

An hour's drive beyond Alwar, the Sariska Tiger Reserve was left without any tigers in 2005, when it was discovered that the park's entire tiger population had vanished, presumably taken by poachers. With a re-population programme, the number of tigers is now believed to be 14. The visitors can also see a wide range of birdlife and a good selection of Indian mammals, ranging from jackals to antelopes.

⑦ Fatehpur Sikri

MAP C3 ▪ Open sunrise–sunset daily ▪ Adm

Around 40 km (25 miles) beyond Agra lie the fascinating remains of the ghost city of Fatehpur Sikri, built by Akbar between 1569 and 1585, but abandoned not long afterwards. The city remains wonderfully preserved, with superb red sandstone buildings and a magically time-warped atmosphere.

⑧ Jaipur

MAP B3

Jaipur, the capital of Rajasthan, is a fascinating city with numerous attractions, ranging from the exuberant bazaars of the old Pink City to the City Palace and the Hawa Mahal, whose five-storey façade is one of India's most famous sights.

Ornate design of Jaipur's Hawa Mahal

⑨ Agra

Once capital of the entire Mughal Empire, the large and chaotic city of Agra is home to some of India's most wonderful and inspiring monuments, including the impressive Agra Fort, the exquisite Itimad-ud-Daulah, Emperor Akbar's Tomb at Sikandra and, of course, the magnificent Taj Mahal (see pp36–9).

The characterful city of Alwar in Rajasthan

⑩ Alwar

MAP B3

Midway between Delhi and Jaipur, the characterful little city of Alwar is considered the traditional northern gateway to Rajasthan. It boasts an imposing fort with ramparts cresting a series of hills above the town, and an absorbing old city palace below.

Delhi Area by Area

Humayun's Tomb, a stunning
example of Mughal architecture

TOP 10 New Delhi

The city of New Delhi, built by the British between 1911 and 1931, still serves as the hub of Delhi's increasingly huge and formless urban expanse. The area divides into two parts. The first is Connaught Place – a huge, vibrant circular plaza of Georgian crescents, that is home to shops, restaurants and other businesses, and is located at the commercial and residential heart of the city. The second, some 2 km (1 mile) south down Janpath, is the great Imperial thoroughfare of Rajpath, linking a triumphalist sequence of Raj-era landmarks, including India Gate and the Rashtrapati Bhavan. The area is also home to almost all the city's finest museums, plus a few relics dating back to the years before British rule.

Sunga Dynasty sculpture, National Museum

AREA MAP OF NEW DELHI

Neo-Classical buildings at Connaught Place

plaza occupies a pivotal position in the layout of the new city, with roads radiating off in every direction. Built around a central park, it is surrounded by colonnaded white Neo-Classical buildings, their shaded arcades hosting shops and restaurants.

1 Connaught Place (CP)
MAP F6 ■ Rajiv Chowk Metro

The commercial hub of New Delhi, Connaught Place, or CP (now officially rechristened Rajiv Chowk), was built between 1929 and 1933 to a design by British architect Robert Tor Russell. The enormous circular

❶	**Top 10 Sights**	see pp77–9
①	**Places to Eat**	see p83
①	**Places to Shop**	see p81
①	**The Best of the Rest**	see p80
①	**Bars and Cafés**	see p82

2 National Museum

This is India's largest and most impressive museum with a vast collection of artifacts from prehistory to the 20th century. Highlights include a superb selection of ancient finds from the Harappan Civilization and an excellent collection of Indian miniatures, alongside Hindu and Buddhist sculpture. Also on display is an array of wonderful Chola bronzes including a famous statuette of the dancing Shiva (see pp32–5).

3 India Gate

At the eastern end of Rajpath stands India Gate, built in 1931 to a design by architect Edwin Lutyens, who also designed the Cenotaph on London's Whitehall. The monument was originally known as the All India War Memorial, built to commemorate the 90,000 soldiers of the British Indian Army killed during World War I and the Afghan Wars. The Tomb of the Unknown Soldier, or Amar Jawan Jyoti, was added in 1971 (see p20).

Imposing India Gate

Observatory at the Jantar Mantar

4 Jantar Mantar
MAP F7 ■ Sansad Marg
■ Janpath Metro ■ Open sunrise–sunset daily ■ www.jantarmantar.org ■ Adm

The Jantar Mantar was one of five outdoor astronomical observatories constructed by the Maharaja of Jaipur, Jai Singh II (the others are in Jaipur, Mathura, Varanasi and Ujjain). Built in 1724, it consists of four huge, strangely shaped stone instruments; these include the Samrat Yantra, a kind of monumental sundial centred on an enormous stone staircase, and the Misra Yantra, shaped like a huge inverted heart. The instruments were designed to perform various functions, including measuring exact solar and lunar calendars and tracking the movements of stars and accurate planetary positions.

5 Rajpath
Originally named Kingsway, Rajpath is the ceremonial axis of Lutyens' New Delhi and links most of the major landmarks of the "new city". It runs all the way from India Gate via Vijay Chowk up Raisina Hill, between the two Secretariat Buildings and on to Rashtrapati Bhavan. The main section, between India Gate and Vijay Chowk, forms Delhi's most impressive open space: a huge sprawling boulevard flanked by lawns, with dramatic views of the Imperial monuments in every direction (see pp20–21).

6 Indira Gandhi Memorial Museum
MAP M5 ■ 1 Safdarjung Road ■ 2301 0094 ■ Open 9:30am–5pm Tue–Sun

Formerly home to both Indira Gandhi and her son, Rajiv, this moving museum is also the site of Indira's assassination (1984) by two of her Sikh bodyguards. There is a wide-ranging array of displays on Indira's years in power, offering a glimpse into both her achievements and lapses into quasi-dictatorship, as well as an extensive collection of Rajiv's personal effects.

CURSE OF THE CITY BUILDERS

An old Persian prophecy claims that "Whoever builds a new city in Delhi will lose it". Several rulers of the city have experienced the force of this curse, but the most spectacular fall from grace was that of the British, who spent around 20 years building New Delhi, only to be forced out within 14 years of the city's completion.

7 Rashtrapati Bhavan
The centrepiece of New Delhi, generally regarded as Lutyens' masterpiece and India's finest example of Colonial-era architecture, is now the residence of the President of India. The work is a remarkable synthesis of Neo-Classical and Indian styles, exemplified by the huge dome, said to have been modelled partly on the Pantheon in Rome and partly on the Buddhist stupa at Sanchi (see p21).

Rashtrapati Bhavan

8 Lakshmi Narayan Mandir

MAP D6 ■ Mandir Marg, near Connaught Place ■ R K Ashram Marg Metro ■ Open 4:30am–noon & 2–9pm daily ■ No cameras or mobile phones allowed

Built in 1938 by industrialist BD Birla, this temple is the biggest and most striking of the various shrines along Mandir Marg, with a clustered mass of red-and-orange *shikharas* (towers) centred on a large marble courtyard. Shrines to Durga and a meditating statue of Shiva stand within.

Lakshmi Narayan Mandir

9 Crafts Museum

Delhi's most entertaining and engaging museum offers an alternative take on the nation's cultural heritage. In contrast to the classic artworks at the National Museum, the emphasis here is on local artisanal traditions, showcasing an incredibly varied – and often quirky – range of cultural, religious and architectural traditions from across the subcontinent (see pp28–9).

10 Gandhi Smriti

MAP N5 ■ 5 Tees January Marg ■ 2301 2843 ■ Open 10am–5pm Tue–Sun ■ www.gandhismriti.gov.in

It was here in 1948 that a Hindu fundamentalist assassinated Mahatma Gandhi. The museum serves simultaneously as an absorbing exposition of Gandhi's life and work and also as a shrine to one of the 20th-century's most inspirational leaders. Stone footsteps mark the route of Gandhi's last walk.

A DAY IN NEW DELHI

▶ MORNING

Begin your day exploring the varied exhibits at the engaging **Crafts Museum** (see pp28–9), then walk along to the eastern end of **Rajpath** and **India Gate** (see p77). Continue on to the **National Museum** (see p77) to spend a couple more hours browsing its superb range of Indian artifacts. Stop for a snack at the museum's small café, or alternatively take an auto-rickshaw down to Khan Market, which has a wide variety of restaurants and cafés from which to choose. Have lunch at **SodaBottleOpenerWala** (see p97) or **Latitude 28 Café** (see p97).

AFTERNOON

Continue walking west along the stately expanse of Rajpath, as Herbert Baker's Neo-Classical **Secretariat Buildings** (see p80) come gradually into view. Carry on to the top of Raisina Hill for a peek at Lutyens' masterpiece, **Rashtrapati Bhavan**; visits can be arranged by calling in advance (see p21). From here, catch an auto-rickshaw, or walk north via **Sansad Bhavan** (see p80), to the 18th-century outdoor astronomical park of **Jantar Mantar**. Take your time inspecting its intriguing planetary instruments, then walk another 100 m (110 yd) north to **Connaught Place** (see p77), the heart of commercial New Delhi. Finish the day with a snack or a drink at one of the area's many restaurants, bars and cafés, such as **1911, Triveni Tea Terrace, Q'BA, Agni, Aqua, ICH** or **Cha Bar** (see p82).

See map on pp76–7 ←

The Best of the Rest

1 Secretariat Buildings

MAP M3 ▪ Raisina Hill

Herbert Baker's grandiose Secretariat Buildings, framing Raisina Hill, are two of the city's finest examples of epic Neo-Classical style.

Crest, Secretariat Buildings

2 Hanuman Mandir

MAP F7 ▪ Baba Kharak Singh Marg ▪ timings vary; check website ▪ www.hanumantempledelhi.com

This temple boasts a richly decorated interior, full of religious atmosphere.

3 Gurudwara Bangla Sahib

MAP E7 ▪ Ashoka Road ▪ Open daily ▪ www.banglasahib.org

The Bangla Sahib is Delhi's most important Sikh *gurudwara* (temple).

4 Agrasen's Baoli

MAP G7 ▪ Off Hailey Road, Kasturba Gandhi Marg ▪ Open daily

This spectacularly deep *baoli* (stepwell), now dry, is thought to have been built by Raja Agrasen (or Ugrasen) in the 14th century.

Agrasen's impressive *baoli*

5 Jawaharlal Nehru Memorial Museum

MAP L5 ▪ Teen Murti Marg ▪ 2341 4666 ▪ Open 10am–5pm Tue–Sun

The former home of India's first prime minister, with a series of period interiors preserved exactly as they were in Nehru's time.

6 National Gallery of Modern Art (NGMA)

MAP Q3 ▪ Jaipur House ▪ 2338 6111 ▪ Open 10am–5pm daily ▪ www.ngmaindia.gov.in

This gallery has an outstanding range of Colonial and modern Indian art.

7 National Philatelic Museum

MAP N2 ▪ Dak Bhawan, Sardar Patel Chowk, Sansad Marg ▪ 2303 6447 ▪ Open 10am–5pm Mon–Fri

A philatelic paradise, with displays covering every stamp issued by India since independence, as well as some older, but well-preserved, exhibits.

8 Sansad Bhavan

MAP M2 ▪ Lok Sabha Marg ▪ Closed to the public

Designed by Lutyens, this edifice is home to the Indian parliament.

9 Cathedral Church of the Redemption

MAP L2 ▪ 1 Church Road, North Avenue ▪ Open 9am–6pm daily

This is Delhi's grandest Anglican church and one of the city's last major Raj-era buildings (1931).

10 St Martin's Church

MAP A6 ▪ Off Cariappa Marg, near Dhaula Kuan and NH8

Built in 1930, this was one of Britain's architectural ventures. It is one of Delhi's most unusual churches.

Places to Shop

(1) The Shop
MAP F6 ■ 10 Regal Building,
Connaught Place ■ 2334 0971 ■ Open
10am–8pm Mon–Sat, noon–7pm Sun
The Shop is an excellent place to buy
beautiful ethnic Indian homewares
and unique lifestyle products.

The Shop, ideal for gifts

(2) People Tree
MAP F6 ■ 8 Regal Building,
Parliament Road, Connaught Place ■
2374 4877 ■ Open 10am–8pm Mon–Sat
Imaginative and colourful apparel
created by a group of artists and
designers committed to social and
environmental causes.

(3) Central Cottage Industries Emporium
MAP F7 ■ Jawahar Vyapar
Bhavan, Janpath ■ 2332 0439
■ Open 10am–7pm daily
This is a government initiative set up
to preserve and develop handicrafts
from all over the country.

(4) Khadi
MAP F6 ■ Khadi Gramodyog
Bhavan, 24 Regal Building,
Connaught Place ■ 2336 0902
■ Open 10:30am–7:15pm Mon–Sat
Another government initiative
supporting the production of Indian
fabrics, natural cosmetics, organic
food, pottery products and hand-
made paper. Ideal for gifts.

(5) Tribes India
MAP F7 ■ Gallery 2, Rajiv
Gandhi Handicrafts Bhavan, Baba
Kharak Singh Marg ■ 2334 1282
■ Open 10:30am–7pm Mon–Sat
A store that stocks some lovely tribal
handicrafts from all over the country.

(6) Soma
MAP F6 ■ K-44
Connaught Place ■ 2341 2966
■ Open 10am–8pm daily
Wonderful dresses, fabrics
and home furnishings, block-
printed by hand using a
traditional Indian method, that
dates from ancient times.

(7) Kamala
MAP F7 ■ Gallery 1,
Rajiv Gandhi Handicrafts
Bhavan, Baba Kharak Singh
Marg ■ 2374 3321 ■ Open
10am–6:30pm Mon–Sat
Kamala offers exotic jewellery, folk
paintings, pottery, bric-a-brac and
handwoven and printed fabrics.

(8) State Emporia Complex
MAP F6 ■ Pallika Kendra, Baba
Kharak Singh Marg ■ Shivaji Stadium
Metro ■ Open 11am–6:30pm Mon–Sat
Visitors can explore and shop from
an array of regional merchandise,
from paintings to crafts, from saris
to jewellery, and much more.

(9) Rikhi Ram
MAP F6 ■ G-8 Connaught Place
■ Open 11:30am–8pm Mon–Sat
Musicians such as the late Ravi
Shankar have bought their sitars and
tablas from this long-established
firm, still crafting traditional musical
instruments the old-fashioned way.

(10) M Ram and Sons
MAP F6 ■ E-21 Connaught
Place ■ Open 10:30am–8pm daily
This excellent tailoring firm, in
business since 1939, can make up
a bespoke suit in no time at all, for a
fraction of department store prices.

See map on pp76–7

Bars and Cafés

The glamorous outdoor space, overlooking the pool, at Aqua

1 Aqua
MAP F7 ■ The Park, 15 Parliament Street ■ 3080 6378 ■ Open noon–12:30pm daily
A glamorous alfresco bar and dining space complete with a pool and chic white-curtained pavilions.

2 Rick's
MAP P4 ■ The Taj Mahal Hotel, 1 Man Singh Road ■ 2302 6162 ■ Open 4pm–1am daily
Everyone's favourite bar in town, Rick's is understated and intimate, and it has an extensive wine list.

3 1911
MAP F7 ■ The Imperial, 1 Janpath ■ 4111 6604 ■ Open 11:30–12:45am daily
Replete with old-world charm, 1911 is best enjoyed on a sunny afternoon over a chilled beer.

4 Triveni Tea Terrace
MAP Q1 ■ Triveni Kala Sangam, Tansen Marg ■ 99715 66904 ■ Open 10am–7:30pm Mon–Sat
Sharing space with four art galleries, this is a charming spot for relaxing.

5 Cha Bar
MAP G7 ■ 148 Barakhamba Road, Statesman House, Connaught Place ■ 2376 6083 ■ Open 9am–6pm Mon–Sat
Housed in the Oxford Bookstore, the Cha Bar offers an extensive tea list.

6 India Coffee House (ICH)
MAP F7 ■ 2nd floor, Mohan Singh Place Shopping Complex, Baba Kharak Singh Marg, off Connaught Place ■ 2334 2994 ■ Open 10pm–1am Wed–Sat
The venerable ICH serves excellent south Indian coffee at low prices.

7 Q'BA
MAP F6 ■ E-42/43 Connaught Place ■ 4517 3333 ■ Open noon–midnight daily
The terrace has fairy lights and a great view of Connaught Place.

8 Agni
MAP F7 ■ The Park, Parliament Street, Connaught Place ■ 2374 3000 ■ Open 5pm–12:30am daily
Loud and fun, Agni is a great place for *bhangra* (Punjabi dance).

9 Legends of India Tea Terrace
MAP F6 ■ N-56 Connaught Place, Outer Circle ■ 4301 2322 ■ Open 12:30–11:45pm daily
This is a charming, old-fashioned spot for afternoon tea, or a beer.

10 Kitty Su
MAP G6 ■ Lalit Hotel, Tolstoy Marg, off Barakhamba Road ■ 3310 5224 ■ Open 10pm–1am Wed–Sat
There is mainly electronic music at this vibrant hotel nightclub with DJs, regular concerts and parties.

Places to Eat

PRICE CATEGORIES

For a meal for one, inclusive of taxes and service charge but not alcohol.

....

₹ under ₹500   ₹₹ ₹500–1,500
₹₹₹ over ₹1,500

 Wasabi by Morimoto
MAP P4 ■ The Taj Mahal Hotel, 1 Man Singh Road ■ 2302 6162 ■ Open 7–11:30pm Mon–Fri, 12:30–2:45pm & 7–11:30pm Sat & Sun ■ ₹₹₹
This swanky restaurant serves excellent Japanese food (see p65).

(2) Andhra Bhawan
MAP P2 ■ 1 Ashoka Road ■ 2338 2031 ■ Open 8–10:30am, noon–3pm & 7:30–10pm daily ■ ₹
The finest spicy Andhra food, served at extremely reasonable prices.

(3) Spice Route
MAP F7 ■ The Imperial, 1 Janpath ■ 2334 1234 ■ Open 12:30–2:30pm & 7–11:30pm daily ■ ₹₹₹
Fine cuisine inspired by places along the Spice Route (see p64).

(4) Veda
MAP F6 ■ H-27 Connaught Place ■ 4151 3535 ■ Open noon–2:30 pm & 6–11:30pm daily ■ ₹₹
An opulent restaurant that serves top-notch food – from the *murgh malai tikka* to Parsi sea bass.

(5) Rajdhani
MAP F6 ■ 9-A Atmaram Mansion, Scindia House, Connaught Place ■ 4350 1200 ■ Open noon–3:30pm & 7–11pm daily ■ ₹
Serving up almost-authentic Gujarati food, this no-frills place is great for a vegetarian thali.

(6) Legends of India
MAP F6 ■ N-56 Connaught Place ■ 4301 2322 ■ Open 12:30–11:45pm daily ■ ₹₹
A quiet place amid the bustle, this serves fairly decent Indian food.

(7) Fire
MAP F7 ■ Park Hotel, 15 Sansad Marg ■ 2374 3000 ■ Open 12:30–2:45pm & 7:30–11:45pm daily ■ ₹₹₹
A smart, contemporary restaurant serving fine modern Indian cuisine, with a seasonal menu, light in summer, fiery hot in winter.

(8) Daniell's Tavern
MAP F7 ■ The Imperial, 1 Janpath ■ 2334 1234 ■ Open 6:30–11:45pm daily ■ ₹₹
This is a lovely, elegant place, inspired by the travels of the late 18th-century artists Thomas and William Daniell, and serving up plates of first-rate Indian cuisine.

(9) Varq
MAP P4 ■ The Taj Mahal Hotel, 1 Man Singh Road ■ 2302 6162 ■ Open 12:30–2:45pm & 7:30–11:30pm daily ■ ₹₹₹
A stylish, relaxed restaurant that serves truly delicious Indian food. Try the lamb cooked in a saffron crust or the excellent crispy Calicut prawns.

Dining space at stylish retaurant Varq

(10) Saravana Bhavan
MAP F7 ■ 46 Janpath ■ 2331 7755 ■ Open 8am–11pm daily ■ ₹
When it comes to authentic South Indian food in Delhi, Saravana Bhavan is the place to go. The mini-tiffin is great (see p64).

See map on pp76–7

🔟 Old Delhi

The city of Shahjahanabad was originally built by Mughal emperor Shah Jahan between 1638 to 1648 to replace the previous Mughal capital of Agra *(see pp36–9)*. Now generally known as Old Delhi, is the most rewarding part of the city. This is Delhi at its most traditional and atmospheric: a fascinating labyrinth of tiny alleyways, colourful bazaars and a profusion of historical monuments and religious shrines, including two of Delhi's landmark attractions: the magnificent Red Fort and the grand Jama Masjid. There are further – albeit more modest – points of interest north of Old Delhi in the quiet Civil Lines district, where the British first established themselves in the city, and along the lush Northern Ridge, where they sought refuge during the opening months of the 1857 Uprising.

Shakti Sthal, Raj Ghat

AREA MAP OF OLD DELHI

Top 10 Sights
see pp85–7

Places to Eat
see p89

The Best of the Rest
see p88

1 Raj Ghat
MAP J5 ■ Mahatma Gandhi Marg ■ Open sunrise–sunset daily

These spacious gardens, set back from the banks of the Yamuna River, are best known as the place where the funeral rites of many of modern India's most important leaders were performed. Most notable among these is perhaps Gandhi, who was cremated here in 1948, and whose simple marble memorial still draws large crowds of reverent visitors. Other memorials dot the lawns, marking the places of the funeral sites of other national leaders, including Shanti Vana (Jawaharlal Nehru), Shakti Sthal (Indira Gandhi) and Vir Bhumi (Rajiv Gandhi).

2 St James' Church
MAP G2 ■ Sham Nath Marg ■ Kashmiri Gate Metro ■ Open 9am–1pm & 2–5pm daily

This little Neo-Classical gem was built by Colonel James Skinner in 1836 – a perfect period piece, constructed in an unusual cruciform pattern with a large dome over the central crossing. In and around the church stand memorials to some of the city's most colourful early British residents, including William Fraser, Thomas Metcalfe (see p27) and Colonel James Skinner himself.

3 Chandni Chowk
Old Delhi's main thoroughfare, and one of the most colourful streets in the city, Chandni Chowk runs dead straight from the gates of the Red

A market stall at Chandni Chowk

Fort due west to the Fatehpuri Masjid (see p15), passing a range of shops and shrines en route. The road's name, meaning Moonlit Square, is said to refer to a square that once stood about halfway along the road, and which was known for the moonlit reflections in the canal that ran through its centre (see pp14–15).

4 Red Fort
The enormous Red Fort served as the residence of the Mughal emperors from its completion in 1648 through to the 1857 Uprising, when the last emperor, Bahadur Shah Zafar II, was exiled to Burma and the British took over the fort, demolishing many of its buildings. What is left now is only a shadow of the original complex, but the surviving pavilions and gardens still give a sense of the sophisticated lifestyles of India's most powerful and cultured rulers (see pp12–13).

The imposing Red Fort

5 Bazaars of Old Delhi

Although much of the physical fabric of Old Delhi is fairly modern – the result of damage sustained during the 1857 Uprising and 20th-century rebuilding – the entire area retains its original, labyrinthine street plan and much of its traditional atmosphere. Different areas are devoted to different trades and crafts – from jewellery and wedding gifts to fireworks and even some spare car parts (see pp66–7).

Atmospheric bazaars of Old Delhi

6 Zinat ul Masjid

MAP J4 ■ Ghata Masjid Road, Daryaganj ■ Taxi or rickshaw ■ Open sunrise–sunset daily

Hidden away in the streets of Daryaganj, this lovely mosque was commissioned in 1707 by Aurangzeb's daughter, Zinat ul Nisa, and is popularly known as the Ghata Masjid. Zinat ul Nisa was buried here in 1711, but her tomb was apparently removed by the British after the Uprising, when the mosque was taken over for military use.

7 Jama Masjid

The Jama Masjid is unquestionably the most beautiful of Old Delhi's Mughal monuments, looming high above the surrounding streets on a natural hillock and dominating all views of the old city. The approach from Meena Bazaar up to the eastern gate, facing the Red Fort, is particularly dramatic, although visitors now have to enter via the rather less imposing gateway on the western side (see pp16–17).

8 Ajmeri Gate

MAP G4 ■ Ajmeri Gate Road ■ Chawri Bazaar Metro

Marooned on a small island amidst busy traffic, this is perhaps the most impressive of the four surviving gateways that once punctuated the old city walls. The fine old *madrasa* and Mosque of Ghazi-ud-Din, built in classic Mughal style, stand just opposite. Elsewhere in the old city, the Delhi, Kashmiri and Turkman gates also survive in good condition – the last is named after the revered Sufi saint, Hazrat Shah Turkman.

Ornate onion domes and arches at the Zinat ul Masjid mosque

The rounded Lal Mandir temple

9 Lal Mandir

Delhi's most important Jain temple, Lal Mandir is located directly opposite the Red Fort, at the southern end of Chandni Chowk. Founded under Shah Jahan for the Jain soldiers in his army, the present building dates from the 1870s. The colourful interior is adorned with dozens of diminutive statues of various Jain *tirthankaras*. The temple's well-known bird hospital stands next door, caring for hundreds of hungry and injured pigeons and other birds, in tiny cages (see p14).

HAZRAT SHAH TURKMAN

Delhi's Turkman Gate is named after a *bayabani* ("jungle dwelling") Sufi hermit, Hazrat Shah Turkman (d. 1240), who lived nearby when the area was still forest. Despite his seclusion, his fame as a holy man spread, and many sought him out. His tiny *dargah* (tomb and mosque) is hidden away in the back alleys. Razia Sultan, a devoted follower of his, was buried nearby.

10 Tomb of Razia Sultan

MAP G4 ■ Off Sitaram Bazaar Road ■ Chawri Bazaar Metro ■ Open sunrise–sunset daily

The tomb occupies an atmospheric roofless enclosure that was built here long before the city that now surrounds it for its proximity to Turkman's tomb. The only female monarch until Queen Victoria to rule a vast swathe of the subcontinent, Razia was loved by the people but hated by the aristocracy, who resented a woman ruler and overthrew her after a four-year reign.

A DAY IN OLD DELHI

MORNING

Start your day at the **Red Fort** (see p85) – arrive early to avoid the crowds. Spend a couple of hours exploring the complex; stop at the food stall outside the main gate for a quick bite. Exit the fort and walk up **Chandni Chowk** (see p85), stopping by the various attractions en route. Stop at **Haldiram's** (see p89), halfway up the road, for a tasty Indian fast-food lunch, then cross the road to **Kanwarji's**, established in 1850 and Delhi's oldest sweet shop since the closure of the famed Ghantewala's, founded in 1790 and once purveyor of sweets to the Mughal emperors.

AFTERNOON

Carry on up Chandni Chowk to the **Fatehpuri Masjid** (see p15), then on to the remarkable spice market of **Khari Baoli** (see p66), just beyond. From here, you can either retrace your steps down Chandni Chowk, then turn right down Dariba Kalan, or alternatively head down Ballimaran to visit the *haveli* of the great Urdu poet Mirza Ghalib (see p88) and then **Chawri Bazaar**, through the heart of Old Delhi's bazaars. Much of the fun lies in simply wandering at will; aim to get lost at least once. Whichever route you take, be at the **Jama Masjid** towards sunset, when this superb mosque is at its most memorable, and the views over the old city and Red Fort are at their best. On leaving the mosque, you will be within a few steps of **Karim's** (see p89), one of Old Delhi's culinary institutions and a perfect spot for an early dinner.

See map on p84

The Best of the Rest

1. Qudsia Bagh
MAP G1 ▪ Lala Hardev Sahai Marg ▪ Open sunrise–sunset daily

These are lovely, peaceful wooded gardens, just north of the old city, and home to a couple of very fine buildings dating back to the gardens' foundation during the 18th century.

Qudsia Bagh

2. Mirza Ghalib Haveli
MAP G3 ▪ Qasimjan Street, off Ballimaran ▪ Open 10am–5pm Tue–Sun

The former home of the great Urdu poet Mirza Ghalib (1797–1869) has been carefully restored and is now a simple museum, with a few exhibits on the writer's life and times.

3. Hauzwali Mosque
MAP G5 ▪ Chandni Chowk ▪ Chandni Chowk Metro ▪ Open sunrise–sunset daily

This little blue mosque is one of the few surviving buildings from the time of Suri ruler Sher Khan.

4. Gauri Shankar Mandir
MAP H3 ▪ Chandni Chowk

One of Old Delhi's largest and most popular Hindu temples (see p15), dedicated to Shiva (Shankar) and Parvati (Gauri).

5. Nicholson's Cemetery
MAP G1 ▪ Lala Hardev Sahai Marg ▪ Open daily

This beautiful, quiet Colonial-era cemetery contains the grave of Brigadier-General John Nicholson, who led the British assault on Delhi in 1857.

6. Pir Ghaib
MAP F1 ▪ Ridge Road ▪ Open daily

Rising up north of Old Delhi is the long, forested Northern Ridge, dotted with British and Tughlaq monuments, such as the ruins of Pir Ghaib, a hunting lodge built by Feroz Shah Tughlaq in the 14th century.

7. Chauburji Masjid
MAP B4 ▪ Magazine Road ▪ Open sunrise–sunset daily

A Tughlaq-era ruins in the Northern Ridge, this structure was built as a tomb around 1345, and subsequently converted into a mosque.

8. Feroz Shah Kotla
MAP J6 ▪ Bahadur Shah Zafar Marg ▪ Open sunrise–sunset daily

All that remains of Sultan Feroz Shah Tughlaq's erstwhile citadel – now popularly thought to be the abode of djinns (spirits).

9. National Gandhi Museum
MAP J5 ▪ Jawaharlal Nehru Marg, opposite Raj Ghat ▪ 2331 0168 ▪ Open 9:30am–5:30pm Tue–Sun (closed Mon & public hols) ▪ www.gandhimuseum.org

At the southern end of the expansive Raj Ghat gardens, this engaging little museum offers some endearingly personal insights into the Mahatma's remarkable life and works.

10. Ashoka Column
MAP E1 ▪ Rani Jhansi Road ▪ Open daily

At the southern end of the Nothern Ridge is one of the city's two Ashokan columns (see p51), from the reign of Ashoka (r. 269–232 BC).

Ashoka Column

Places to Eat

PRICE CATEGORIES

For a meal for one, inclusive of taxes and service charge but not alcohol.
....
₹ under ₹500 ₹₹ ₹500–1,500
₹₹₹ over ₹1,500

1 Karim's
MAP H4 ▪ 16 Gali Kababiyan, Matia Mahal, Jama Masjid ▪ 2326 4981 ▪ Open 9am–12:45pm daily ▪ ₹
This Delhi institution has been doling out delicious Mughlai food for over half a century (see p65).

2 Gujarati Samaj
MAP F1 ▪ 2 Raj Niwas Marg, Civil Lines ▪ 2398 1796 ▪ Open 6am–10:30am, 11:30am–3pm & 7pm–10:30pm daily ▪ ₹
A family-run restaurant that serves delicious, fuss-free Gujarati food.

3 Haldiram's
MAP G3 ▪ 1454/2 Chandni Chowk ▪ 4768 5111 ▪ Open 9am–11pm daily ▪ ₹
Good Indian street food and sweets prepared in hygienic conditions.

4 Moti Mahal
MAP H5 ▪ 3703 Netaji Subhash Marg, Daryaganj ▪ 2327 3661 ▪ Open 11:30am–midnight daily ▪ ₹₹
Dating back to Independence, this restaurant claims to have invented the famous butter chicken.

5 Embassy Restaurant
MAP G1 ▪ 13 Alipur Road, Civil Lines ▪ 2399 3061 ▪ Open noon–11:30pm daily ▪ ₹₹
A delightful old-world restaurant reminiscent of Colonial clubs, serving standard North Indian fare.

6 The Curzon Room
MAP G1 ▪ Oberoi Maidens, 7 Sham Nath Marg, Civil Lines ▪ 2397 5464 ▪ Open 12:30–2:30pm & 7:30–11:45pm daily ▪ ₹₹₹
Dig into the sumptuous lunch buffet at this elegant Raj-style restaurant.

7 The Garden Terrace
MAP G1 ▪ Oberoi Maidens, 7 Sham Nath Marg, Civil Lines ▪ 2397 5464 ▪ Open daily 7am–11pm ▪ ₹₹
Spilling into a lovely courtyard, The Garden Terrace, part of the venerable Maidens Hotel, is an ideal place for nursing a cup of coffee.

8 Paranthe Wali Gali
MAP G3 ▪ Opposite Natraj Restaurant, 1396 Chandni Chowk ▪ Open 11am–11pm daily ▪ ₹
The "alley of parantha-makers" is a real foodie's delight, offering an overwhelming variety of this delicious stuffed Indian bread.

Old-style charm at Chor Bizarre

9 Chor Bizarre
MAP H5 ▪ Hotel Broadway, 4/15A Asaf Ali Road ▪ 4366 3600 ▪ Open noon–3pm & 7:30–10:45pm daily ▪ ₹₹
One of the oldest restaurants in Old Delhi, Chor Bizarre is famous for its superb Kashmiri cuisine (see p64).

10 Kake di Hatti
MAP G3 ▪ 654 Church Mission Road, Fatehpuri, Chandni Chowk ▪ 99107 22254 ▪ Open 8am–1am daily ▪ ₹
This place draws flocks of locals to mop up its legendary daal makhni.

Following pages The Diwan-i-Aam audience hall at Delhi's Red Fort

TOP10 South of the Centre

The area south of New Delhi, now home to some of the city's most upmarket suburbs, boasts a superb swathe of Mughal (and some Sultanate) monuments. At the top of most visitors' lists is the magnificent Humayun's Tomb, the first great masterpiece of Mughal architecture, though there are also stand-out attractions nearby at the wonderfully atmospheric religious enclave of Nizamuddin, the beautiful parklands and historic monuments of the Lodi Gardens, Safdarjung's Tomb, and the rugged citadel of Purana Qila, while just across the Yamuna River lies Akshardham Temple, India's most extravagant modern Hindu shrine.

Khan-i-Khanan's Tomb

① Khan-i-Khanan's Tomb
MAP R7 ■ Mathura Road, south of Humayun's Tomb ■ Open sunrise–sunset daily ■ Adm

This grandiose tomb is the burial place of Abdur Rahim, Akbar's prime minister, who died in 1626, although it may have been built for his wife, who died in 1598. The tomb has four grand *iwans* and a bulbous central dome surrounded by *chattris*, rather like a sketch for the Taj Mahal minus the minarets.

AREA MAP OF SOUTH OF THE CENTRE

① **Top 10 Sights**
see pp92–5

① **Places to Eat**
see p97

① **Places to Shop**
see p96

2 Purana Qila
MAP R3 ■ Mathura Road
■ Pragati Maidan Metro ■ Open
sunrise–sunset daily ■ Adm

The sixth city of Delhi, the Purana
Qila *(see p51)* was begun by
Humayun and completed by his rival
Sher Shah Suri. Its large, rugged
walls stretch for over a mile and
enclose a large swathe of parkland
dotted with various buildings. The
two most notable are the imposing
Qala-i-Kuhna Masjid, and the more
delicate Sher Mandal, an unusual
octagonal pavilion that was used by
Humayun as a library and observatory.

A baby hippo at the Zoological Park

3 National Zoological Park
MAP R4 ■ Mathura Road, near
Purana Qila ■ Pragati Maidan Metro
■ Open Apr–Oct: 9am–4:30pm Sat–
Thu; Nov–Mar: 9am–4pm Sat–Thu;
closed Fri ■ Adm ■ www.nzpnew
delhi.gov.in

The largest in India, Delhi's popular
zoo is home to around 2,000 animals,
including national treasures such as
rhinos, elephants and Bengal tigers,
and a good selection of wildlife from
the Americas, Australia and Africa.

Spread out over expansive parkland,
it provides a pleasant, sympathetic
environment for its captive animals,
as well as a peaceful refuge for the
city's human population. It is also a
great spot for a weekend picnic.

4 Lodi Gardens
The beautiful Lodi Gardens
are among Delhi's most attractive
retreats, offering a beguiling combination of nature and culture, with an
idyllic wooded landscape dotted with
fine tombs dating from the Lodi and
Sayyid dynasties *(see pp30–31)*.

Safdarjung's Tomb, set in a *charbagh*-style garden

⑤ Safdarjung's Tomb

MAP M6 ▪ Airforce Golf Course, at the intersection of Safdarjung Road & Aurobindo Marg ▪ Taxi, auto-rickshaw or Jor Bagh Metro ▪ Open sunrise–sunset daily ▪ Adm

This mausoleum was built in 1754 for Safdarjung (1708–54), the Nawab of Awadh and one of the most important Mughal nobles during the reigns of Muhammad Shah and Ahmad Shah Bahadur. A good example of late-Mughal design, the tomb is a large and floridly decorated sandstone structure with a bulbous dome set in a *charbagh*-style garden.

LAST RITES, DELHI-STYLE

No other city in the world boasts as copious a range of mausoleums as Delhi – from certain angles the city can look like a kind of enormous necropolis. Oddly enough, such buildings run directly contrary to Koranic orthodoxy, which forbids the construction of elaborate funerary monuments – a prohibition that was ignored by the city's rulers.

---

⑥ Akshardham Temple

MAP C5 ▪ Taxi or Akshardham Metro ▪ Open 9:30am–6:30pm Tue–Sun ▪ Electronic equipment not allowed ▪ www.akshardham.com

Opened in 2005, this is perhaps the largest and most spectacular modern Hindu temple in India. The huge complex is centred on an extravagant shrine, ringed by 148 elephant statues; inside is an impressive-looking golden figure of Bhagwan Shri Swaminarayan, in whose honour the temple was built. The temple hosts exhibitions and even has a fountain water show at sunset.

⑦ Nizamuddin

MAP R6 ▪ Taxi or Jangpura Metro (Hazrat Nizamuddin metro is scheduled to open in 2017) ▪ Open 24 hrs ▪ Hope Project reservations: 2435 7081

This atmospheric religious enclave grew up around the tomb of the great Sufi saint Sheikh Nizamuddin Auliya (1238–1325), and is busy with pilgrims at all hours, with performances of devotional *qawwali* singing after dark. It is also home to a cluster of Mughal monuments and the graves of various

Objects on sale at Nizamuddin

notable individuals, including poet and musician Amir Khusrau (1253–1325), Shah Jahan's daughter Jahanara and the great Urdu poet Mirza Ghalib (see p88). Hope Project, a local NGO, runs evening walking tours of the adjoining Nizamuddin village, a fascinating way to learn about the area.

8 National Rail Museum
MAP U1 ▪ Satya Marg, Chanakyapuri ▪ Dhaula Kuan Metro ▪ 2688 1816 ▪ Open 9:30am–5:30pm Tue–Sun ▪ Adm and charge for video and train rides

This museum is a shrine to India's fascination with all things pertaining to the train. Among the highlights are the lavish carriages of local and foreign royals, including the Prince of Wales and the Maharaja of Mysore.

Locomotive, National Rail Museum

9 Khair ul Manazil Masjid
MAP Q4 ▪ Mathura Road, opposite Purana Qila ▪ Pragati Maidan Metro ▪ Open sunrise–sunset daily

Just across the road from the Purana Qila lies the impressive, though now rather derelict, Khair ul Manazil Masjid, built in 1562 by Maham Anga, the powerful wet-nurse of Akbar. The mosque is a classic example of early Mughal architecture, its low and rather stocky façade reminiscent of the earlier Sultanate style.

10 Humayun's Tomb
One of the greatest of all Mughal garden tombs, this superb mausoleum is one of Delhi's finest monuments and a magnificent memorial to the personable but erratic Humayun, the second Mughal emperor (see pp18–19).

A DAY SOUTH OF THE CENTRE OF DELHI

▶ MORNING

It is possible to see most of the major sights covered in this section in one long, albeit very busy, day. Note that you will need to pick up auto-rickshaws to get between them, or hire a taxi or auto-rickshaw for the day. The highlights of the **Akshardham Temple** can be seen in two hours, but for a more leisurely visit, allow half a day. Alternatively, you could pick from the following selection for a more relaxed tour.

Start your day at the imposing **Safdarjung's Tomb**, then walk a short distance down the road to the **Lodi Gardens** (see p93). Explore the various tombs that dot the beautiful parkland – don't miss the lovely bonsai garden. Take lunch at the **Lodi Garden Restaurant** (see p31) or at the classy **Basil and Thyme** (see p97) in nearby **Sunder Nagar**.

AFTERNOON

Take an auto-rickshaw to the brooding **Purana Qila** (see p93), then cross the road to visit the **Khair ul Manazil Masjid**. From here, you can get another auto-rickshaw down to **Humayun's Tomb** (see p18). Explore the tomb and gardens and the other mausoleums that dot the vast complex, then walk across the road to the wonderful little *dargah* at **Nizamuddin**. For dinner you could head to the nearby **Baci** or **Perch** (see p97), before or after attending the evening *qawwali* session at the *dargah*.

See map on pp92–3

Places to Shop

1 The Bookshop
MAP N7 ▪ 13/7 Main Market, Jor Bagh ▪ 2469 7102

The Bookshop is lovingly stocked with a wide range of reading matter, from well-thumbed classics to pristine new arrivals.

2 Dilli Haat
MAP V1 ▪ Opposite INA Market ▪ 2611 9055 ▪ Adm

A daily open-air market run by Delhi Tourism, with several stalls selling wonderful arts and crafts – not to mention food – from every single state in India.

3 Good Earth
MAP P5 ▪ 9-ABC Khan Market ▪ 2464 7175

This luxurious store stocks a range of exclusively designed dining products, high-quality linen and some lovely home-decor items.

4 Mittal Tea House
MAP P7 ▪ 8-A Lodi Colony Market ▪ 2461 5709

The pleasant Mittal Tea House stocks beautifully packed Darjeeling, Assam and Nilgiri teas, as well as Kangra and Kashmiri green teas.

5 Bharany's
MAP R4 ▪ 14 Sundar Nagar Market ▪ 2435 8528

Bharany's takes pride in every one of its handcrafted jewellery items. It also has a fine collection of textiles.

Amrapali bracelet

6 Silverline
MAP P5 ▪ 7-A Khan Market ▪ 2464 3017

The walls of this busy shop are lined with beautiful jewellery in antique, ethnic and contemporary designs.

7 Amrapali
MAP P5 ▪ 39 Khan Market ▪ 4175 2024

The exclusive collection here includes exquisite contemporary jewellery, designer, enamel, ethnic and antique pieces.

8 Ladakh Jeweller's
MAP R4 ▪ 10 Sundar Nagar Market ▪ 2435 5424

A lovely shop that specializes in beautiful ethnic Indian handcrafted jewellery in gold and silver.

9 Ogaan Closet
MAP P5 ▪ 77 Khan Market ▪ 4175 7220

This shop has a splendid ensemble of clothes, accessories and jewellery by various Indian designers. It also provides a platform for Indian design and stocks some luxurious clothes that are exquisite in cut and design.

10 Anokhi
MAP P5 ▪ 32 Khan Market ▪ 2460 3423

Specializing in contemporary crafted textiles with roots in Jaipur, Anokhi stocks ethnic and western wear.

Anokhi's colourful designs

Places to Eat

PRICE CATEGORIES

For a meal for one, including taxes and
service charge but not alcohol.

₹ under ₹500   ₹₹ ₹500–1,500
₹₹₹ over ₹1,500

 OTW (On the Waterfront)
MAP Q6 ▪ The Lodhi, Lodi Road
▪ 4363 3333 ▪ Open noon–3pm &
7–11:45pm daily ▪ ₹₹₹
The OTW exudes chic style and serves
excellent Asian and European cuisine.

 Perch
MAP P5 ▪ 71, 1st Floor,
Khan Market ▪ 83739 76637 ▪ Open
11:30am–1:30am daily ▪ ₹₹₹
A sophisticated coffee and wine
bar with great European cuisine.
The coffee sangria is a must try.

3 Baci
MAP R4 ▪ 23 Sundar Nagar
Market ▪ 4150 7445 ▪ Open 11am–
midnight daily ▪ ₹₹
One of the most charming spots in
town, Baci has a strong Italian menu.

 Basil and Thyme
MAP R4 ▪ 28 Sunder Nagar
Market ▪ 4378 7722 ▪ Open
11am–11pm daily ▪ ₹₹
Run by Bhicoo Manekshaw, the first
Indian woman to have completed
the advanced Cordon Bleu cookery
course, this airy restaurant offers
good European cuisine.

5 Latitude
MAP P5 ▪ Good Earth,
Khan Market ▪ 2462 1013 ▪ Open
11am–11pm daily ▪ ₹₹₹
A stylish café that focuses on great
contemporary dishes with a twist.

6 Bukhara
MAP K5 ▪ ITC Maurya, Sardar
Patel Marg ▪ 2611 2233 ▪ Open 12:30–
2:45pm & 7–11:45pm daily ▪ ₹₹₹
This is one of the world's top Indian
restaurants, serving superb North-
West Frontier cuisine (see p65).

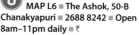
Dum Pukht's glamorous dining room

7 Dum Pukht
MAP K5 ▪ ITC Maurya, Sardar
Patel Marg ▪ 2611 2233 ▪ Open
7am–11:45pm daily ▪ ₹₹₹
Slow-cooked *dum* (steam casserole)
dishes from Lucknow, served amidst
tastefully glitzy surroundings.

8 Sagar Ratna
MAP L6 ▪ The Ashok, 50-B
Chanakyapuri ▪ 2688 8242 ▪ Open
8am–11pm daily ▪ ₹
This place serves simple, delicious
vegetarian South Indian meals.

9 Coast Café
MAP U2 ▪ H-2, Hauz Khas
Village ▪ 3310 5045 ▪ Open noon–
1am daily ▪ ₹₹
With classy interiors, this restaurant
serves curries from the coasts of
India and varieties of fish and chicken
stews. Cocktails are delicious too.

10 SodaBottleOpenerWala
MAP P5 ▪ 73 Khan Market,
Subramaniam Bharti Marg ▪ 3310
5665 ▪ Open 11:30am–11pm daily
▪ ₹₹
A quirky, old-fashioned Bombay
Parsi restaurant, successfully
re-created in Delhi (see p65).

See map on pp92–3

🔟 South Delhi

The upwardly mobile suburbs of South Delhi are where visitors will find what makes modern Delhi tick, with a string of upmarket neighbourhoods, suave restaurants and glitzy modern malls. Despite its contemporary appearance, however, South Delhi was home to the city's earliest settlements, and boasts many of its most atmospherically time-warped monuments. Most of these

Baha'i Temple

date back to the Delhi sultans, whose various forts, mosques and wonderful mausoleums still stand scattered majestically amongst modern suburbia. The highlight is the extraordinary Qutb Minar complex and the adjacent Mehrauli Archaeological Park, while there are further memorable attractions at both Tughlaqabad and Hauz Khas.

AREA MAP OF SOUTH DELHI

- **1** Top 10 Sights
  see pp99–101
- **1** Places to Eat (Indian)
  see p104
- **1** Places to Eat (Global)
  see p105
- **1** Places to Shop
  see p102
- **1** Bars and Cafés
  see p103

RAO TULA RAM MG
SANGAM MG
MAHATMA GANDHI ROAD (RING ROAD)
SAROJINI NAGAR
INA Ⓜ
SOUTH EXTENSION

Hyatt Regency Hotel
TAMIL SANGAM MG
AFRICA AVENUE
GREEN PARK
Ⓜ AIIMS 7

600 metres
VASANT VIHAR
Basant Lok Market
OLOF PALME MARG
Deer Park
BABA GANGANATH MG

Ⓜ Green Park
Hauz Khas Village
Shahpur Jat Market
SIRI FORT
AUGUST

NELSON MANDELA MARG
Jawaharlal Nehru University
SHAHEED JEET SINGH MARG
Sanjay Van
ARUNA ASAF ALI MARG
AUROBINDO MARG

Hauz Khas
GAMAL ABD
PANCHSHEEL PARK
GEETANJALI MARG
MALVIYA NAGAR
PRESS ENCLAVE MARG
SAKET

VASANT KUNJ
ABDUL GAFFAR KHAN MARG
BABU JAGJIVAN RAM ROAD
MEHRAULI VILLAGE
ANUVRAT MARG
MEHRAULI BADARPUR ROAD
NEB SARAI ROAD

Malviya Nagar Ⓜ
Ⓜ Saket
MANDIR

Ⓜ Qutab Minar
Garden of Five Senses

0 kilometres   2
0 miles   1

1 Baha'i Temple

MAP X2 ▪ Kailash Colony
▪ Open summer: 9am–6:30pm Tue–Sun; winter: 9am–5pm Tue–Sun
▪ www.bahaihouseofworship.in

Completed in 1986 to a design by Iranian architect Fariborz Sahba, the Baha'i Temple is Delhi's most striking modern building. Popularly known as the Lotus Temple, the design was inspired by the image of an unfolding lotus flower, with 27 huge white petals emerging from nine pools, symbolizing the nine spiritual paths of the Baha'i faith.

2 Tomb of Sultan Ghari

MAP T3 ▪ Abdul Gaffar Khan Marg, Vasant Kunj ▪ Taxi or auto-rickshaw ▪ Open 24 hrs

Marooned on the outskirts of the city, this impressive but little-visited tomb was built in 1231 by Iltutmish for his son and heir Nasiruddin Mahmud following the latter's premature death. It is the oldest Islamic tomb in India, looking more like a fort than a mausoleum. The name Sultan Ghari means "Royal Cave", referring to the troglodytic burial chamber beneath the central octagonal platform. The tomb is an architectural curiosity, as much Hindu as Muslim in style.

3 Quwwat-ul-Islam

The centrepiece of the Qutb Minar complex, the Quwwat-ul-Islam was the subcontinent's first mosque, begun by Aibak and extended by his successors, including Alauddin Khilji *(see p45)*, who added the fine Alai Darwaza red sandstone gateway in 1311. Inside, the prayer-hall screen, covered in Koranic carvings, is one of India's finest early examples of Islamic architecture *(see p24)*.

4 Qutb Minar

One of Delhi's most iconic sights, the soaring Qutb Minar towers over the southern city: a vast minaret begun during the reign of the first Delhi sultan Qutbuddin Aibak. The design is quite unlike anything else in the subcontinent, more Afghan than Indian, with angular projecting flanges punctuated by balconies and bands of Koranic script *(see pp24–5)*.

Column detail at Qutb Minar

Domes at Begumpuri Masjid

5 Begumpuri and Khirki Masjids

MAP V2 ■ Off Guru Govind Singh Road ■ Hauz Khas or Malviya Nagar Metro ■ Open sunrise–sunset daily

These mosques are typical of their 14th-century Tughlaq era, the Begumpuri with its arcaded courtyard topped by domes, the Khirki with its tapering shape and almost completely covered courtyard.

6 Mehrauli Village and Archaeological Park

MAP U3 ■ Anuvrat Marg, south of the Qutb Minar ■ Open sunrise–sunset daily

The Mehrauli Archaeological Park and adjacent village of Mehrauli are home to an extraordinary collection of ancient monuments, dating from the 13th to the 19th centuries. There is a rich cluster of Mughal monuments, ranging from the Jamal-Kamali Masjid to the Zafar Mahal, and notable Sultanate-era attractions such as the Jahaz Mahal and the serene *dargah* of the Sufi saint Qutb Sahib, buried away in the depths of the village (see pp26–7).

7 Ashoka's Rock Edict

MAP X2 ■ Off Raja Dhirsain Marg ■ Open 24 hrs

Not far from the Baha'i Temple lies a large boulder, carved with a faint tracery of fading Brahmi script. This is one of the city's three monuments dating from the time of the Mauryan Emperor Ashoka (see p51). Ashoka converted to Buddhism early in his reign, and erected, across the country, a series of pillars and rock edicts on which his various proclamations were recorded. Unlike the city's two Ashokan columns, this rock edict stands on its original site.

8 Hauz Khas Village

MAP U2 ■ Hauz Khas Village ■ Taxi, auto-rickshaw or Green Park Metro ■ Open 24 hrs

The upmarket village of Hauz Khas is home to a string of ancient monuments, the Deer Park (see p56) and a number of eating and shopping venues. The village is centred around a reservoir, the Hauz-i-Alai, built by Alauddin Khilji in 1304. The sequence of buildings girding the lake was added half a century later.

Monuments at Mehrauli Village

URBAN VILLAGES

Scattered amid South Delhi's suburbs are the remains of many formerly isolated villages that have now been swallowed up by the advancing urban tide. The most notable ones are Nizamuddin, Chiragh and Mehrauli. Each is home to an important *dargah* and retains its original street layout.

9 Chiragh Delhi
MAP W2 ■ Off Gamal Abdel Nasser Marg ■ Taxi or auto-rickshaw

Now engulfed by suburban sprawl, the ancient village of Chiragh Delhi has managed to preserve much of its traditional atmosphere, retaining parts of the walls that once surrounded it. The main attraction here is the *dargah* of Roshan Chiragh Delhi, while the tomb of Delhi sultan, Buhlul Lodi, lies outside the village.

Citadel ruins at Tughlaqabad

10 Tughlaqabad
MAP X3 ■ Mehrauli-Badarpur Road ■ Taxi, auto-rickshaw or Badarpur Border Metro ■ Open sunrise–sunset daily ■ Adm and charge for video

Constructed during the reign of Ghiyasuddin Tughlaq *(see p50)*, Tughlaqabad was the third city of Delhi, dwarfing the previous settlements of Siri and Lal Kot, with a string of fortified ramparts and city walls stretching for 6 km (4 miles). The walls and citadel within are now largely ruined, but still impressive. Just over the road lies the austere tomb of Ghiyasuddin himself.

A DAY IN SOUTH DELHI

▶ MORNING

South Delhi's attractions are spread out, and you will need to take transport between the various sites. You could pick up auto-rickshaws between each stop, though it is easiest to hire a knowledgeable taxi- or auto-rickshaw-driver for the day to ferry you around the various sites.

Start the day with an hour or so at the remarkable **Qutb Minar Complex** *(see p99)* and spend the rest of the morning exploring the monuments of the **Mehrauli Archaeological Park** and the adjacent **Mehrauli Village**. Next, head to the excellent **Garden of Five Senses** *(see p56)* and have lunch at **Olive Bar & Kitchen** *(see p105)*.

AFTERNOON

After lunch, head north, taking in some of Delhi's least-visited but most absorbing monuments, including the **Begumpuri Masjid**. Stop in the fascinating urban village of **Chiragh Delhi** to visit the *dargah*. If you have time, visit the **Khirki Masjid** and nearby **Lal Gumbad** *(see p44)*. Then, drive over towards **Hauz Khas**. Visit the beautiful reservoir and surrounding buildings, the Deer Park, and then explore the quiet streets of Hauz Khas Village and its superb boutique shops. Continue north to the **Baha'i Temple** *(see p99)*, aiming to arrive in the evening when the lighting makes it look spectacular. Finally, make your way back to Nehru Place to the International Trade Tower for a meal at **Oh! Calcutta** *(see p104)*.

See map on pp98–9

Places to Shop

(1) Shahpur Jat Market
MAP V2 ▪ Shahpur Jat, Siri Fort
▪ Open daily (shop hours vary)

Vintage and contemporary clothing, accessories, jewellery, rugs and home decor are all on offer in the trendy new fashion boutiques of this chic urban village *(see p63)*.

(2) Kilol
MAP W2 ▪ 6-N Block Market, Greater Kailash I ▪ 2924 3388
▪ Open 10am–8pm Wed–Mon

A lovely store specializing in hand-block-printed, reasonably priced fabrics from Jaipur.

(3) Tatsat
MAP U2 ▪ E-50 Main Market, Hauz Khas ▪ 4165 5792 ▪ Open 10am–8pm Mon–Sat, noon–8pm Sun

Tatsat sells garments, accessories, recycled goods, stationery and colourful hand-painted *chai* glasses and kettles, all sourced from eco-friendly organizations.

(4) DLF Emporio
MAP T2 ▪ 4 Nelson Mandela Marg, Vasant Kunj ▪ 4611 6666
▪ Open 11am–9pm daily

Delhi's most deluxe shopping mall, where affluent Delhiites come to buy designerwear from all the top international brands.

(5) Ravissant
MAP X1 ▪ 50–51 Community Centre, New Friends Colony ▪ 2683 7278 ▪ Open Mon–Sat ▪ www.ravissant.in

A sophisticated store with beautiful "Indian-inspired" clothes in breezy fabrics, home decor and silverware.

(6) Abraham & Thakore
MAP W1 ▪ Moonriver Building, D-16 Defence Colony ▪ 98717 74436
▪ Open Mon–Sat ▪ www.abraham-andthakore.com

A Delhi fashion institution best known for its classic cuts and pristine natural fabrics.

(7) Nalli
MAP V1 ▪ D-2 South Extension II
▪ 2462 9926 ▪ Open 10am–8:30pm daily

Established in 1928, Nalli is popular for its traditional and exquisite silk saris in lovely colours and patterns.

(8) Utsav Boutique
MAP W2 ▪ 3 Krishi Vihar Complex ▪ 2624 2420 ▪ Open 11am–7:30pm Mon–Sat

Utsav stocks saris in every possible fabric imaginable, plus accessories.

Exquisite Fabindia furnishings

(9) Fabindia
MAP W2 ▪ 7 N Block Market, Greater Kailash I ▪ 2923 2183 ▪ Open 10am–8pm daily

Fabindia stocks everything from furniture and natural cosmetics to organic food and clothes.

(10) Zaza
MAP W2 ▪ 25–26 Community Centre, Zamrudpur ▪ 4105 2525
▪ Open 10am–8pm daily

A lovely lifestyle store filled with beautiful furniture, brightly coloured linen, unusual cutlery and covetable home-decor products.

Bars and Cafés

1 Polo Lounge
MAP U1 ■ Hyatt Regency, Bhikaji Cama Place ■ 2679 1234 ■ Open 11am–1am daily

Step back in time at this plush, England-inspired bar.

2 Kylin
MAP T1 ■ 24 Basant Lok, Vasant Vihar ■ 95820 01010 ■ Open noon–midnight daily

With fantastic cocktails, this is ideal for a lazy drink at lunch or a lively evening with friends.

3 Social
MAP U2 ■ 9-A & 12, Hauz Khas Village ■ 3310 5944 ■ Open 11am–1am daily

A popular restaurant-bar that serves a range of global dishes, creative cocktails and some of the best breakfasts in Delhi.

4 The Piano Man
MAP V2 ■ B-6-7/22 Safdarjung Enclave Market ■ 4131 5181 ■ Open noon–3pm & 7pm–12:30am daily

This club, with a grand piano and an intimate bar, is a great place for live jazz performances and cocktails.

5 Monkey Bar
MAP T2 ■ Plot 11 Upper Ground Floor, LSC, Pocket C-6 & 7, Vasant Kunj ■ 3310 6238 ■ Open noon–12:30am daily

A hip new bar with a touch of the gastropub and great cocktails.

6 Lord of the Drinks Forum
MAP W2 ■ Epicuria Mall, Nehru Place Metro Station ■ 3310 5723 ■ Open 11am–12:45am daily

With great ambiance and incredible music, this place offers a selection of innovative drinks and cocktails.

7 Shalom
MAP W2 ■ 18 N Block Market, Greater Kailash I ■ 4163 2280 ■ Open 12:30–3:30pm & 7:30pm–midnight daily

Live music, paired with cool Mediterranean decor and great cocktails, make Shalom one of the city's most popular nightclubs.

8 Café Intermezzo
MAP W1 ■ 34 Defence Colony Market ■ 2433 8119 ■ Open 10am–10pm daily

A quiet, friendly, home-style café with changing art displays on the walls.

9 PCO
MAP T3 ■ Near PVR Priya Cinema ■ 4606 2444 ■ Open 5:30pm–12:30am daily

A "speakeasy", with a secret entry code, retro decor and exotic cocktails.

10 Café Turtle
MAP W2 ■ 16 N Block Market, Greater Kailash I ■ 2924 5641 ■ Open 10:30am–8:30pm daily

A relaxed, friendly café atop the lovely Full Circle bookstore.

Coffee and books at Café Turtle

See map on pp98–9

Places to Eat (Indian)

1 Swagath
MAP W1 ▪ 14 Main Market, Defence Colony ▪ 2433 0930 ▪ Open 11am–midnight daily ▪ ₹₹

Swagath is known for serving some of the most delicious South Indian fare in town.

2 Oh! Calcutta
MAP W2 ▪ HA-1 International Trade Tower, Nehru Place ▪ 3040 2415 ▪ Open noon–3:30pm & 7:30–11:30pm daily ▪ ₹₹

Exuding old-world charm, this restaurant specializes in excellent traditional Bengali fare.

Indian Accent's cosy interior

7 Indian Accent
MAP X2 ▪ Manor Hotel, 77 Friends Colony ▪ 4323 5151 ▪ Open noon–3pm & 7–11pm daily ▪ ₹₹₹

A swanky yet cosy venue that offers finely prepared local dishes (see p64).

3 Carnatic Café
MAP X1 ▪ Community Centre, New Friends Colony ▪ 4100 8630 ▪ Open 9am–10:30pm daily ▪ ₹

Innovative dosas and fabulous filter coffee, served at reasonable prices.

8 Zaffran
MAP W2 ▪ 2 N Block Market, Greater Kailash I ▪ 3310 5215 ▪ Open noon–3:30pm & 7:30pm–midnight daily ▪ ₹₹

A stylish terrace space serving up plates of simple but delicious food.

4 Sagar
MAP W1 ▪ 18 Defence Colony Market ▪ 2433 3658 ▪ Open 8am–11pm daily ▪ ₹

A friendly canteen-style place, with reasonably priced, delicious vegetarian South Indian cuisine.

9 Punjabi by Nature
MAP T1 ▪ 11 Basant Lok, Vasant Vihar ▪ 4611 7000 ▪ Open noon–11:30pm daily ▪ ₹₹

This friendly restaurant is most famous for its vodka gol gappas (puffed flour crisps that are filled with cumin-spiced water).

5 Dakshin
MAP V3 ▪ Sheraton New Delhi Hotel, District Centre, Saket ▪ 4266 1122 ▪ Open 12:30–3pm & 7:30–11:30pm daily ▪ ₹₹₹

Elegant and unassuming, this place serves the best Malayali food in the city.

Authentic Malayali cuisine at Dakshin

10 Potbelly Rooftop Cafe
MAP V2 ▪ 116-C, 4th Floor, Shahpur Jat ▪ 4161 2048 ▪ Open noon–11pm daily ▪ ₹

The authentic Bihari cuisine served at this rooftop restaurant includes litti chokha – a roasted dough ball stuffed with sattu (roasted chickpea flour), served with mashed roast aubergine and potato.

6 Delhi Club House
 MAP U1 ▪ Sangam Courtyard, R K Puram ▪ 97175 35533 ▪ Open noon–12:30am daily ▪ ₹₹

This restaurant-bar offers a curated selection of signature dishes from clubhouses across India.

Places to Eat (Global)

PRICE CATEGORIES
For a meal for one, inclusive of taxes and service charge but not alcohol.
....
₹ under ₹500 ₹₹ ₹500–1,500
₹₹₹ over ₹1,500

1 The China Kitchen
MAP U1 ■ Hyatt Regency, Bhikaji Cama Place ■ 2679 1234 ■ Open noon–2:30pm & 7–11:30pm daily ■ ₹₹₹

A culinary milestone when it comes to Chinese food in the city, complemented with stylish interiors *(see p65)*.

2 Hungry Monkey
MAP V2 ■ B–6/6 DDA Market, opposite Deer Park, Safdarjung Enclave ■ 4604 9801 ■ Open 12:30pm–12:30am daily ■ ₹

The Hungry Monkey's terrace comes complete with its own bar, canopies and lots of greenery, and the menu is inspired by California cuisine.

3 Diva
MAP W2 ■ M-8A, M Block Market, Greater Kailash II ■ 2921 5673 ■ Open 11am–midnight daily ■ ₹₹

This quiet, understated restaurant serves arguably the best Italian food in town. Sunday brunch is popular.

4 Qla
MAP U3 ■ 4-A, Seven Style Mile, Kalka Das Marg, Kila, Mehrauli ■ 3007 9200 ■ Open noon–midnight Wed–Mon ■ ₹₹₹

This fine-dining restaurant serves European-influenced cuisine in an old *haveli* (mansion). The lovely courtyard is ideal for sunny brunches and atmospheric dinners; the terrace has great views of the Qutb.

5 Olive Bar & Kitchen
MAP U3 ■ One Style Mile, Haveli 6, Mehrauli ■ 2957 4444 ■ Open 12:30am–12:30pm daily ■ ₹₹₹

Located in an atmospheric old *haveli*, Olive serves up excellent light Italian and Mediterranean fare *(see p64)*.

6 Tamura
MAP V2 ■ S-16 Green Park Extension Market ■ 2653 5868 ■ Open noon–3pm & 6–10pm daily ■ ₹₹

This cosy restaurant serves excellent home-style Japanese fare.

7 Smoke House Deli
MAP U2 ■ 12 Hauz Khas Village ■ 2656 7001 ■ Open 10:30–1am daily ■ ₹₹

A modern European restaurant that focuses on smoked and grilled meats.

8 Lebanese Point
MAP V3 ■ Shop 7 Ground Floor, PVR Anupam Shopping Complex, Saket ■ 4166 4440 ■ Open noon–11:30pm daily ■ ₹

The best chicken shawarmas in town; decent falafel and mezze, too.

9 La Piazza
MAP U1 ■ Hyatt Regency, Bhikaji Cama Place ■ 2679 1234 ■ Open noon–2:30pm & 7–11:30pm daily ■ ₹₹

Fresh, hearty Italian dishes amid relaxed, rustic surroundings.

10 Fio Cookhouse & Bar
MAP W2 ■ Epicuria Mall, Nehru Place Metro Station ■ 3310 7873 ■ Open noon–12:30am daily ■ ₹₹₹

Largely European and Indian cuisine, along with inventive cocktails that are concocted using the principles of molecular gastronomy.

Fio, great for pizza and drinks

Top 10 Delhi
Streetsmart

Auto-rickshaws parked in New Delhi

Getting To and Around Delhi

Arriving by Air

The city's **Indira Gandhi International Airport** has two terminals – T3 handles international and some domestic flights (carriers include **Air India, Air Canada, Jet Airways, British Airways, Virgin Atlantic** and **United Airlines**), and T1 is used for low-cost domestic flights (airlines include **IndiGo, SpiceJet** and **Go Air**). There are currently direct flights to Delhi from all major hubs, including London, Toronto, New York and Sydney.

The fastest way into town from T3 is via the Airport Express Link (5am–11pm) of the Delhi Metro, which takes 20 minutes to reach New Delhi rail station (Ajmeri Gate side). From T1 there's a connecting shuttle (6am–10pm) to Delhi Aerocity station.

A 24-hour bus service connects both terminals to Connaught Place, New Delhi Station (Ajmeri Gate side), the Red Fort and Maharana Pratap ISBT (40 minutes).

For taxis, there are pre-paid taxi kiosks in the arrivals area, but prices vary, so check a few.

Arriving by Train

The most convenient railway station for most visitors is New Delhi, which, despite its name, is located between New Delhi and Old Delhi. Some services from northern India use Delhi Junction at the northern end of Old Delhi. Many services from the south (including some from Agra) use Hazrat Nizamuddin, south of the centre near Nizamuddin village, while those from the east may terminate at Anand Vihar, and those from Rajasthan terminate at Sarai Rohilla.

New Delhi and Anand Vihar have metro stations, while Delhi Junction is served by Chandni Chowk metro. The metro station at Hazrat Nizamuddin is scheduled to open in 2017. All rail terminals have kiosks for pre-paid auto-rickshaw fares.

For the city of Agra, the most convenient service is the 6am Bhopal Shatabdi Express from New Delhi, returning from Agra Cantonment station at 9.15pm.

Stations are a hotspot for theft; always keep an eye on your baggage, and beware of anyone trying to distract your attention.

Foreign tourists should buy their tickets from the **Foreigners' Booking Office** on the upper floor of New Delhi station (bring your passport). Staff can advise on the best trains to use, or you can check the **Indian Railways** website for timetables or call the **Railway Enquiries** phone number. It's best to ignore anyone who tells you that the office has closed or volunteers directions to it (almost certainly with the intention of directing you to a crooked travel agent).

Arriving by Road

The main intercity bus station is **Maharana Pratap ISBT** (Intercity State Bus Terminal) in Old Delhi, served by the Kashmiri Gate metro station. Some use **Anand Vihar ISBT** (Anand Vihar metro station), while **Rajasthan Roadways** buses arrive at **Bikaner House** near India Gate.

Travelling by Metro and Bus

The **Delhi Metro**, which runs from 5am until midnight, is the most convenient way of getting around town. Trains run every two to four minutes, and tickets are cheap. Rechargeable Smart Cards save time and are worth getting if you intend to use the metro during your trip. The one-day Tourist Card is not good value. Women have reserved seats, as well as the whole first carriage to themselves, which it is wise to use, especially during peak hours. Baggage is limited to 15 kg (33 lb), or 60 cm x 45 cm x 25 cm (23.5 in x 17.5 in x 10 in).

DTC (Delhi Transport Corporation) has a good bus network. Routes can be confusing, and vehicles may be very crowded, but at times the service can be very handy. Their website can tell you the best route between any two bus stops, but you will need to know the correct names for the stops.

Travelling by Taxi

To hail a taxi you'll need to haggle, so know in advance how much you want to pay. Your hotel should be able to book you a cab, but otherwise it's best to take one from a local stand. Metered radio cabs are a good option, but they cost a little more – **Meru Cabs, Mega Cabs,** and **Quick Cabs** can be booked online, by phone, or via their apps. **Ola** and **Uber** are booked via their apps.

Travelling by Auto-Rickshaw

Auto-rickshaws ("autos") are the standard way of getting around Delhi. Autos are fitted with meters, but most drivers won't use them and you'll probably have to haggle. Know what price you want to pay before stopping an auto, and agree a fare before setting off. Fares should be ₹19 for the first kilometre then roughly ₹6.50 per kilometre. You can avoid having to haggle (and ensure you don't get overcharged) by hiring pre-paid autos at official set rates from kiosks in Connaught Place, at Janpath (outside the tourism office) and at major transport terminals.

Travelling by Cycle Rickshaw

Cycle rickshaws are a great way to get around the old city. Fares are about half those of an auto, but again, haggling is the order of the day. Cycle rickshaws are banned from Connaught Place and central New Delhi. Rickshawwallahs are among Delhi's poorest: if they do a good job, be generous.

Tours

DTTDC runs a range of tours in town and out, including a one-day city tour, and **DTC** also runs one-day city tours by bus. **HoHo** has hop-on hop-off bus tours, and **Delhi by Cycle** runs 3.5-hour cycle tours.

DIRECTORY

ARRIVING BY AIR

Air Canada
📞 4717 2900
🌐 aircanada.com

Air India
📞 1 800 180 1407
🌐 airindia.in

British Airways
📞 0124 417 3777
🌐 britishairways.com

Go Air
📞 2566 2111
🌐 goair.in

IndiGo
📞 92127 83838
🌐 goindigo.in

Indira Gandhi International Airport
📞 0124 337 6000
🌐 newdelhiairport.in

Jet Airways
📞 3989 3333
🌐 jetairways.com

SpiceJet
📞 98718 03333
🌐 spicejet.com

United Airlines
📞 0124 431 5500
🌐 united.com

Virgin Atlantic
📞 0124 469 3030
🌐 virgin-atlantic.com

ARRIVING BY TRAIN

Foreigners' Booking Office
New Delhi Railway Station, Upper Floor; 8am–8pm Mon–Sat, 8am–2pm Sun
📞 2336 6177

Indian Railways
🌐 indianrail.gov.in

Railway Enquiries
📞 2336 6177
🌐 enquiry.indianrail.gov.in/ntes

ARRIVING BY ROAD

Anand Vihar ISBT
📞 2215 2431

Maharana Pratap ISBT
📞 2386 8694

Rajasthan Roadways, Bikaner House
📞 2338 3469

TRAVELLING BY METRO AND BUS

Delhi Metro
📞 2341 7910
🌐 delhimetrorail.com

DTC
📞 2331 7600
🌐 dtcbusroutes.in

TRAVELLING BY TAXI

Mega Cabs
📞 4141 4141
🌐 megacabs.com

Meru Cabs
📞 4422 4422
🌐 merucabs.com

Ola Cabs
🌐 olacabs.com

Quick Cabs
📞 6767 6767
🌐 quickcabs.in

Uber
🌐 uber.com/cities/new-delhi

TOURS

Delhi by Cycle
📞 6464 5906
🌐 delhibycycle.com

DTC
📞 2375 2772 ext 244
🌐 dtc.nic.in

DTTDC
📞 2336 3607
🌐 delhitourism.gov.in

HoHo
🌐 hohodelhi.com

Practical Information

Passports and Visas

Everybody (except those from Nepal and Bhutan) needs a visa to enter India. Nationals of most countries, if arriving at Delhi airport with an onward or return ticket, can get a 30-day tourist visa online before their departure. For a longer stay, you'll need to apply in person or by post at the nearest **Visa Office** or alternatively at the Indian High Commission – there is a list of the latter on the website of the **Ministry of External Affairs**. It's best to allow plenty of time. Your passport should be valid for at least six months beyond your arrival date. The **UK, US, Canada, Australia, New Zealand** and many other countries have consular representation in the city.

Travel Safety Advice

Visitors can get up-to-date travel safety information from the **UK Foreign** and **Commonwealth Office**, the **US Department of State** and the **Australian Department of Foreign Affairs and Trade**.

Customs and Immigration

Duty-free limits are two litres of liquor, and 200 cigarettes or 50 cigars or 200g tobacco.

Travel Insurance

Don't travel without valid insurance, and check the details of the policy, particularly how much you can claim for the loss of individual items. For medical treatment you may have to pay upfront and claim it back later.

Health

Vaccinations against meningitis, typhoid, tetanus as well as hepatitis A are commonly recommended for India, and you should make sure that you are covered against polio. Exactly what you need will depend on where you are going, so consult your doctor well before your trip. Malaria and dengue fever outbreaks can occur, especially in and after the monsoon months (July–September), so bring high-DEET repellent and protect yourself against mosquito bites.

Stick to bottled drinking water (or purify your own) and avoid food left lying out – the busier and more popular the restaurant, the safer it is likely to be. Street food can play havoc with those who have delicate constitutions, and ice cream, salads, juices and fruit are all notorious germ-carriers. The most common tourist illness is "Delhi belly" – a stomach upset that passes within a day or two (stick to water, yoghurt and rice). If your symptoms persist, it's a good idea to consult a doctor, in case it's giardia or amoebic dysentery. **AIIMS** (All India Institute of Medical Sciences) is one of the country's top research hospitals; other well-known hospitals include **Dr Ram Manohar Lohia Hospital**, the **East West Medical Centre**, and the **Apollo Hospitals** chain. The **US Embassy Delhi Doctors List** is also useful. The **Apollo Pharmacy** in Connaught Place is open 24 hours.

Personal Security

Mugging and violent crime against tourists is rare, but petty theft such as pickpocketing and pilfering from hotel rooms is quite common, as is credit-card fraud. If you are paying with plastic, ensure that it is swiped in front of you and that the card never leaves your sight.

Transport terminals are particular hotspots for theft. There have been instances of travellers being offered drugged food or drink and then robbed once insensible, so never accept food or drinks from strangers, especially while at transport terminals.

Most hotels have a safe for valuables, although it is not unknown for things to go missing from cheap hotels. It is often better to use your own padlock to lock your baggage or even the room.

Sexual harrassment of women ("eve teasing") is unfortunately quite rife, especially in crowds. The best response is to point out the perpetrator and explain in a loud voice exactly what he has done, as other people will be on your side. Violent attacks on women occasionally occur, so exercise caution after dark. Dressing conservatively and wearing a wedding ring may help. If you need to contact the police, call the police's **Tourist Helpline** or their **Women's Helpline**; the tourist police also have posts at the airport, main stations, major tourist sights and hotel areas. There are also dedicated numbers for **ambulances**, **fire brigade** and the **police**.

Travellers with Special Needs

The city isn't particularly accessible for the disabled, but things are improving. Old Delhi in particular is hard-going in a wheelchair, although New Delhi, with its wider pavements (and cow ban) is easier. The airport and metro stations are fully accessible to travellers with special needs. Major sights such as the National Museum, Crafts Museum, Qutb Minar and the Red Fort make some effort, with ramps and disabled-access toilets; the HoHo tour buses *(see p109)* also have disabled access.

Sources of Information

India Tourism and **Delhi Tourism** have offices off Connaught Place, and Delhi Tourism has offices at the airport and bus and railway stations.

Delhi Diary, which is free at the India Tourism office, lists exhibitions and cultural events, while **Time Out Delhi** has entertainment listings. Online, check out **Delhi Capital**, **Little Black Book** and **India for You**.

DIRECTORY

PASSPORTS AND VISAS

Australian High Commission
🔳 india.embassy.gov.au

British High Commission
🔳 ukinindia.fco.gov.uk

Embassy of Canada
🔳 india.gc.ca

Embassy of the United States
🔳 newdelhi.usembassy.gov

Ministry of External Affairs
🔳 mea.gov.in

New Zealand High Commission
🔳 nzembassy.com/india

Visa Office, Australia
🔳 vfsglobal.com/india/australia

Visa Office, Canada
🔳 blsindia-canada.com

Visa Office, UK
🔳 vfsglobal.com/India/UK

Visa Office, USA
🔳 in.ckgs.us

TRAVEL SAFETY ADVICE

Australian Department of Foreign Affairs and Trade
🔳 dfat.gov.au

🔳 smartraveller.gov.au

UK Foreign and Commonwealth Office
🔳 gov.uk/foreign-travel-advice

US Department of State
🔳 travel.state.gov

HEALTH

AIIMS
Aurobindo Marg
📞 6590 0669
🔳 www.aiims.edu

Apollo Hospitals
🔳 www.apollohospdelhi.com

Apollo Pharmacy
G-8 Connaught Place
📞 2371 1838

Dr Ram Manohar Lohia Hospital
Baba Kharak Singh Marg
📞 2340 4286
🔳 rmlh.nic.in

East West Medical Centre
38 Golf Links
📞 2469 9229
🔳 eastwestrescue.com

US Embassy Delhi Doctors List
🔳 in.usembassy.gov/u-s-citizen-services/local-resources-of-u-s-citizens/doctors

PERSONAL SECURITY

Ambulance
📞 102
Fire Brigade
📞 101

Police
📞 100 or 1090

Tourist Helpline
📞 87508 71111

Women's Helpline
📞 1091

SOURCES OF INFORMATION

Delhi Capital
🔳 delhicapital.com

Delhi Diary
🔳 delhidiary.in

Delhi Tourism
Coffee Home, Baba Kharak Singh Marg, opp the Hanuman Temple
📞 2336 5358
🔳 delhitourism.gov.in

India for You
🔳 indfy.com/delhi

India Tourism
88 Janpath; open 9am–6pm Mon–Fri, 9am–2pm Sat
📞 2332 0005
🔳 incredibleindia.org

Little Black Book
🔳 lbb.in/delhi

Time Out Delhi
🔳 timeout.com/delhi

Currency and Banking

The local currency is rupees (₹), which come in notes of ₹2,000, ₹500, ₹100, ₹50, ₹20, ₹10 and occasionally still ₹5, with coins of ₹10, ₹5, ₹2, ₹1 and 50 paise. It is illegal to import or export Indian currency, and, if you have over US$10,000 in foreign currency, you must declare it.

Banks are usually open 10am to mid-afternoon Monday to Friday, plus a couple of hours on Saturday mornings. Private bureaux de change are becoming quite common, especially in Connaught Place and Paharhanj, and may offer decent rates. Mid- and upper-range hotels exchange foreign currency, but rates are usually poor. ATMs are widespread and accept foreign-issued credit and debit cards (especially Visa and MasterCard). These two types of credit card are widely accepted in upmarket shops and restaurants, but they may attract a surcharge.

Telephone and Internet

International and national phone calls can be made easily and relatively cheaply from numerous telephone booths (look for places advertising STD/ISD phone calls). Calls can often be made from hotel rooms, but there may be an extortionate mark-up, so check rates first. The country code for India is +91; the area code for Delhi is 011.

If you are planning to use your mobile in Delhi, check rates and accessibility with your service provider at home. Alternatively, buy a local SIM card (available at phone shops), for an Indian telephone number and access to cheap local phone rates.

Most hotels provide Wi-Fi access, and many bars and cafés provide free Wi-Fi, there are also a few free Wi-Fi zones in the city. For internet cafés try **Sunrise** and **Cyber Floor** at Connaught Place.

Postal Services

There is a handy branch of the **Post Office** at Connaught Place. For poste restante, you will need to go to the **General Post Office (GPO)**, also near Connaught Place. Sending letters and postcards is easy, but packages do need to be sealed.

TV, Radio and Newspapers

Most hotel rooms in Delhi will have a TV offering local and international channels. Local FM radio stations, including **Zabardast Hit FM, Red FM, Radio City** and **Radio Mirchi**, play mostly Hindi pop; **Radio One** plays a more international selection. The national radio station, **All India Radio**, has three daily news bulletins in English, and the **BBC World Service** can be picked up in the evenings.

India's English-language press includes newspapers **The Times of India** (whose local edition has the useful Delhi Times supplement) and **Hindustan Times**, the left-leaning **The Hindu**, and the **Indian Express**. **India Today** is an English-language television network that is broadcast 24 hours a day.

Opening Hours

Shops typically open 10am–6pm Monday to Saturday. Many museums and some tourist sights are closed on Mondays.

Time Difference

Delhi is on India Standard Time (IST), which is 5.5 hours ahead of London, 9.5 hours ahead of New York, 12.5 hours ahead of Los Angeles, and 4.5 hours behind Sydney.

Electrical Appliances

The electricity supply is 230V 50Hz AC. Most sockets are triple round-pin but take European-size double round-pin plugs. British, Irish and Australasian devices will need only an adaptor, while North American devices will need an adaptor and a converter.

Weather

The best times to visit are spring (February–April) and autumn (mid-September–November). Delhi can be extremely hot in May and June (reaching 45°C/113°F), rather wet from late June until mid-September, when the monsoon kicks in, and decidedly chilly in December and January, when temperatures can dip below 5°C (41°F). Bring a jacket and sweater if you are travelling during these months.

Shopping

A wide array of crafts from all over India is available in Delhi. The **State Emporia Complex** *(see p67)* on Baba Kharak Singh Marg has fixed, marked prices and is the best places to start looking, while the **Crafts Museum** shop *(see pp28–9)* and **Dilli Haat** *(see p96)* also have excellent selections. Even if you don't buy anything, it's worth visiting to check prices and quality before heading elsewhere. Bargaining is de rigueur in bazaars and most small shops, but not usually in malls and government emporiums.

Delhi is brilliant for clothes, from upmarket but still affordable local chains such as **Anokhi** *(see p96)* and **Fabindia** *(see p102)* to bargain offerings in clothing bazaars such as **Katra Neel** *(see p67)* off **Chandni Chowk** *(see pp14–15)*.

Hundreds of shops sell textiles by the metre, so buy some fabric and have your clothes tailored at affordable prices.

Other top buys include accessories such as belts, bags and jewellery; home decor; natural cosmetics; tea and spices, especially at **Khari Baoli** market *(see p66)*; books (the city has some excellent book-shops); and Bollywood film posters, which curio shops in **Hauz Khas Village** have at bargain prices *(see p67)*.

Dining

Delhi has a vibrant food scene. Vegetarians are particularly well catered for. The Indian staple of paneer (cottage cheese) is a good alternative to meat in curries. Particularly in Agra be sure to sample Mughlai cuisine, largely non-vegetarian, with creamy, delicately spiced sauces, dried fruit and nuts. In south Indian restaurants, a *thali* is a

good option, consisting of a selection of curries plus rice and breads. The city's Tibetan colony at **Majnu ka Tila** *(see p60)* is a great place for Tibetan food.

The restaurants are child-friendly, and if children find spicy food hard to deal with, there are many alternatives including cafés, Chinese eateries, international chains and multi-cuisine restaurants among others. **Haldiram's** *(see p89)* is child-friendly.

Where to Stay

Delhi has a huge range of accommodation, from five-star hotels to cheap backpacker lodges. Rates for mid-range accom-modation are a bargain by Western standards. **Airbnb** is very useful for locating unique places to stay. **Couchsurfing**, which allows travellers to book to stay with a family for a short period, is also available in Delhi.

DIRECTORY

TELEPHONE AND INTERNET

Cyber Floor
17 Scindia House,
Connaught Place
85859 78587

Sunrise
N-9/2,
Near SONY Showroom,
Connaught Place
92129 35568

POSTAL SERVICES

General Post Office (GPO)
Patel Chowk on Sansad Marg at Ashoka Road

Post Office
A-6 Connaught Place;
10am–7pm Mon–Sat

TV, RADIO AND NEWSPAPERS

All India Radio
1368kHz MW
W allindiaradio.gov.in

BBC World Service
1413kHz MW

Hindustan Times
W hindustantimes.com

Indian Express
W indianexpress.com

India Today
W indiatoday.com

Radio City
91.1MHz FM
W planetradiocity.com

Radio Mirchi
93.5MHz FM
W radiomirchi.com

Radio One
94.3MHz FM
W radioone.in

Red FM
93.5MHz FM
W redfmindia.in/delhi

The Hindu
W thehindu.com

The Times of India
W timesofindia.com

Zabardast Hit FM
95.0MHz FM
W hit95fm.in

WHERE TO STAY

Airbnb
W airbnb.com

Couchsurfing
W couchsurfing.com

Places to Stay

Luxury Hotels

The Claridges
MAP N5 ▪ 12 Dr APJ
Abdul Kalam Road ▪ 3955
5000 ▪ www.claridges.
com/hotels/the-clarid
ges-new-delhi ▪ ₹₹
A landmark in Lutyens's
Delhi, Claridges is the
epitome of old-world
style. The building, with
Colonial-style pillars and
high ceilings, houses 137
rooms and suites and has
great restaurants. Guests
will find it difficult to
leave, as did The Beatles,
when they stayed in 1968.

Hyatt Regency
MAP U1 ▪ Bhikaji Cama
Place ▪ 2679 1234 ▪ www.
delhi.regency.hyatt.com
▪ ₹₹
The Hyatt is ideal for
travellers who like to feel
the vibrant pulse of the
city. The imposing struc-
ture houses a flamboyant
lobby space, stylish and
spacious rooms, a sleek
club lounge and some
excellent restaurants.

ITC Maurya
MAP K4 ▪ Diplomatic
Enclave, Sardar Patel
Marg ▪ 2611 2233 ▪ www.
itchotels.in ▪ ₹₹–₹₹₹
Nestled in greenery, this
is a delightful accommo-
dation option due to its
impeccable service, loca-
tion, forested Ridge views
and excellent restaurant,
Bukhara (see p65). It also
houses beautiful artworks
from eminent artists.

The Lalit
MAP G6 ▪ Barakhamba
Avenue, Connaught Place
▪ 4444 7777 ▪ www.
thelalit.com ▪ ₹₹
Rooms are stylish and
modern at this sleek five-
star just a five-minute
walk from Connaught
Place. It is also home to
the chic nightclub Kitty
Su (see p82).

Oberoi Maidens
MAP G1 ▪ 7 Sham Nath
Marg ▪ 2397 5464
▪ www.maidenshotel.
com ▪ ₹₹– ₹₹₹
Built in the early 1900s
and nestled close to the
city's leafy Civil Lines
area, this beautiful white
heritage building, with
its Colonial architectural
style, still retains a strong
old-world charm.

The Park
MAP F7 ▪ 15 Parliament
Street ▪ 2374 3000
▪ www.theparkhotels.
com ▪ ₹₹
Contemporary art and
design are the highlight
of this hotel's decor, but
the impeccable service
and chic, spacious rooms
are welcome additions.
Unwind at Aqua, the
poolside restaurant set
around a swimming pool.

The Taj Mahal Hotel
MAP P4 ▪ 1 Man Singh
Road ▪ 6656 6162
▪ www.taj.tajhotels.com
▪ ₹₹–₹₹₹
A gorgeous lobby with
Art Deco marble floors,
fountains and beautiful
mini-domes greets
visitors to this hotel. The
Taj's rooms are just as
impressive, with decor
that is a blend of trad-
itional and contemporary.

Vivanta by Taj –
Ambassador
MAP P5 ▪ Sujan Singh
Park, Subramaniam
Bharti Marg ▪ 6626
1000 ▪ www.vivanta.
tajhotels.com/en-in/
ambassador-new-delhi
▪ ₹₹–₹₹₹
Comfortable and stylish
rooms, with classic
interiors, at this centrally
located hotel. The many
highlights of staying here
include a fitness centre
that offers yoga, a popular
on-site restaurant and a
lovely breakfast buffet.

The Imperial
MAP F7 ▪ 1 Janpath ▪ 2344
1234 ▪ www.theimperial
india.com ▪ ₹₹₹
Opened in 1931, the
Imperial is considered
one of Asia's finest hotels.
From its sweeping palm–
lined drive to its classical
white Colonial structure,
the place exudes quiet
elegance and luxury. The
walls are lined with a fine
collection of European
"traveller" paintings.

The Lodhi
MAP Q6 ▪ Lodi Road
▪ 4363 3333 ▪ www.
thelodhi.com ▪ ₹₹₹
Starting off as part of the
luxury Aman chain, the
Lodhi is now an indepen-
dent hotel. The hotel
combines modern decor
with traditional touches
such as Lodi-inspired jali
screens and Khareda

stone floors. The hotel has a great spa and even offers Turkish *hammam* and private plunge pools. Suites with excellent views of the city.

The Taj Palace
MAP K4 ■ 2 Sardar Patel Marg, Diplomatic Enclave ■ 2611 0202 ■ www.tajhotels.com ■ ₹₹₹
This grand building is nestled within lovely lawns and has striking interiors. Relax at the nine-hole chip-and-putt golf green or work out at the state-of-the-art fitness centre.

Boutique Hotels

Amarya Villa
MAP V1 ■ A-2/20 Safdarjung Enclave ■ 4175 9267 ■ www.amaryagroup.com ■ ₹₹
Conveniently located, this hotel is set away from the bustling crowds. It offers a range of spacious and stylish guestrooms that have been themed around the "Navratna", India's nine traditional auspicious gemstones.

B Nineteen
MAP S6 ■ B-19 Nizamuddin (East) ■ 98710 88629 ■ www.bnineteen.com ■ ₹₹
A gorgeous boutique hotel, this blends tasteful contemporary style with traditional decor and lovely wooden furniture. The service is non-intrusive, the food excellent and the location is top notch.

Colonel's Retreat
MAP W1 ■ D-418 Defence Colony ■ 4660 4927 ■ www.colonelsretreat.com ■ ₹₹
Calling itself Delhi's "best-kept secret", this charming accommodation option feels a bit like staying in a friend's home. The terrace is the perfect place to relax and read a book or enjoy a meal.

Haveli Dharampura
MAP G4 ■ 2293 Gali Guliyan, Dharampura, near Jama Masjid Gate No. 3, Chandni Chowk ■ 4603 5500 ■ www.welcomheritagehotels.in/hotel-details/Haveli-Dharampura ■ ₹₹
Set in an 1887 *haveli*, this is a wonderfully atmospheric hotel located in the bustling alleys of Old Delhi's Chandni Chowk, a short walk from the Jama Masjid and the Red Fort. The rooms are beautiful and the service is excellent.

Haveli Hauz Khas
MAP U2 ■ P-5 Hauz Khas Enclave ■ 4165 1357 ■ www.havelihauzkhas.com ■ ₹–₹₹
Located in the peaceful Hauz Khas Enclave residential colony, this hotel boasts five rooms, each one decorated according to a different theme, ranging from Hampi to Ajanta. One of the highlights of the place is the pleasant rooftop lounge area for guests.

Hotel Diplomat
MAP K4 ■ 9 Sardar Patel Marg, Diplomatic Enclave ■ 4605 0200 ■ www.thehoteldiplomat.com ■ ₹₹
Set amid sprawling green lawns, this hotel offers tastefully decorated rooms with contemporary interiors. The on-site restaurant, with a bistro vibe, is multi-cuisine and offers all-day breakfast and a view of the gardens.

Jaypee Vasant Continental
MAP T2 ■ Vasant Vihar ■ 2614 8800 ■ www.jaypeehotels.com/vasant-continental-new-delhi ■ ₹₹
Strategically located, the hotel blends business and leisure and offers modern accommodation. Amenities at the hotel include a swimming pool, health spa, fitness centre and a range of dining options.

jüSTa Panchsheel Park
MAP V2 ■ S-362 Panchsheel Park ■ 4058 2121 ■ www.justahotels.com/panchsheel-park-new-delhi ■ ₹₹
The 22 airy rooms at the hotel have beautiful handcrafted Burmese teak furniture and superb contemporary art on the walls. It's the perfect home away from home.

Lutyens Bungalow
MAP N6 ■ 39 Prithviraj Road ■ 2469 4523 ■ www.lutyensbungalow.co.in ■ ₹₹
Constructed in 1937, this charming bungalow is located in plush Central Delhi, strolling distance from Lodi Gardens and Safdarjung's Tomb. There is a swimming pool to relax and the living room is furnished with books and a fireplace for cool winter evenings.

The Manor
MAP X1 ■ 77 Friends Colony (West) ■ 4323 5151 ■ www.themanordelhi.com ■ ₹₹
This opulent hotel is situated in a quiet corner of the upmarket colony. It houses Indian Accent, a lovely restaurant known for its great fusion cuisine.

The Muse
MAP W2 ▪ A-1 Chirag Enclave ▪ 4065 0000 ▪ www.musedelhi.com ▪ ₹₹
Though not nearly as atmospheric as most boutique hotels in this city, the Muse is excellent for business travellers as it is located close to the Nehru Place commercial complex. Their rooms are stylish and minimalist.

Roseate House
MAP A6 ▪ Asset #10, Hospitality District, Aerocity ▪ 7155 8800 ▪ www.roseatehotels.com/newdelhi ▪ ₹₹
Located close to the airport, this hotel offers beautiful rooms and excellent service. Guests can relax at the outdoor and indoor spa, enjoy at the movie lounge or shop at the luxury brand stores.

La Sagrita
MAP R4 ▪ 14 Sundar Nagar ▪ 4150 7013 ▪ www.lasagrita.com ▪ ₹₹
The rooms at this small but swanky boutique hotel are spacious and cool. The breakfast is excellent, and the neighbourhood is quiet and compact, tucked away between India Gate and the grand Humayun's Tomb.

Scarlette
MAP U1 ▪ B2-139 Safdarjung Enclave ▪ 95820 79058 ▪ www.scarlettenewdelhi.com ▪ ₹₹
This *maison d'hôte* offers four lovely rooms with French interiors blended with modern decor. It is the personal touch of the two French owners that makes this place stand out from other hotels.

Thikana
MAP V2 ▪ A-7 Gulmohar Park ▪ 98115 43335 ▪ www.thikanadelhi.com ▪ ₹₹
Enjoy a comfortable stay at this hotel that offers rooms with ethnic decor and earthy tones. The common areas have comfortable chairs, ideal for sinking into with a book or a drink.

Mid-Range Hotels

Bajaj Indian Homestay
MAP E5 ▪ 8A/34 Karol Bagh ▪ 2573 6509 ▪ www.indianhomestay.com ▪ ₹
The clean and spacious rooms at this homestay are named after Hindu gods as well as other mythological characters. There is also a charming terrace with views.

BB Palace
MAP E5 ▪ 2638 Bank Street, Gurudwara Road, Karol Bagh ▪ 4761 3500 ▪ www.hotelbbpalace.com ▪ ₹
A friendly place with a few pleasant rooms. Ask to see the rooms before booking – those decorated with bright colours and dark wood furniture are lovely.

Bloomrooms Hotel
MAP R7 ▪ 7 Link Road, Jangpura Extension ▪ 4122 5666 ▪ www.bloomrooms.com ▪ ₹
This is a great option located nearby popular sights such as Humayun's Tomb and the Lodi Gardens.The rooms are pleasant with minimalist decor in cheerful yellows and whites. Amici Café has a set-up here and serves all-day breakfast.

Devna
MAP R4 ▪ 10 Sundar Nagar ▪ 2435 5047 ▪ www.devnadelhi.com ▪ ₹
Surrounded by greenery and located in a lovely neighbourhood, this guesthouse offers rooms decorated with antiques and paintings. There is a state-of-the-art gymnasium next door.

Hamilton Hotel
MAP V2 ▪ S–153 Panchsheel Park ▪ 2601 5852 ▪ ₹
Located at the edge of Panchsheel Park, the Hamilton is ideally situated for exploring South Delhi's sights. The rooms are done up in bright colours, and there is a charming porch with a fountain where guests can unwind on comfortable cane chairs.

Hotel Broadway
MAP H5 ▪ 4/15-A Asaf Ali Road ▪ 4366 3600 ▪ www.hotelbroadwaydelhi.com ▪ ₹
Dating back to 1956 and sandwiched between Old Delhi and Connaught Place, Hotel Broadway has a certain endearing charm. The friendly staff can arrange activities for you, ranging from performances of traditional dance to walking tours through the old city.

Hotel Florence
MAP E5 ▪ 2719 Bank Street, Karol Bagh ▪ 4714 4714 ▪ www.florencegroup.in ▪ ₹
A decent hotel offering comfortable rooms with clean en-suite bathrooms. An in-house restaurant serves Indian and some European dishes.

Ahuja Residency
MAP Q5 ▪ 193 Golf Links ▪ 2461 1027 ▪ www.ahujaresidency.com ▪ ₹₹
Located in one of the city's most upmarket residential quarters, this is a good option for a quiet, relaxing stay. Efficient, non-intrusive service, beautiful room decor that blends the contemporary with the traditional, a cosy dining space and all modern amenities, make Ahuja Residency a great place to stay for a few days.

Hotel Palace Heights
MAP F6 ▪ D-26/28 Connaught Place ▪ 4358 2610 ▪ www.hotelpalaceheights.com ▪ ₹₹₹
Tastefully decorated rooms with lovely paper blinds and warm, woody colours, an excellent restaurant and a great location are among the few reasons to stay at Palace Heights. The terrace restaurant is great for a beer and peppery *chicken tikka*.

Ibis
MAP A6 ▪ Asset #9, Hospitality District, Delhi Aerocity ▪ 4302 0202 ▪ www.ibishotels.com ▪ ₹₹₹
Set near the airport, this chain hotel offers comfortable rooms with modern amenities. They also have a sumptuous breakfast buffet.

Budget Hotels

Blue Triangle Family Hostel (YWCA)
MAP E7 ▪ Ashoka Road ▪ 2336 5441 ▪ www.ywcaofdelhi.org ▪ ₹
This hostel provides safe and clean accommodation, particularly for women. There is a choice of double or single rooms, with en-suite baths and running hot water.

FabHotel Casa Friends Colony
MAP X1 ▪ Mint Casa, A-10, Friends Colony (East) ▪ 4242 4242 ▪ www.fabhotels.com ▪ ₹
The hotel has modern, comfortable rooms and efficient service. It is well located for exploring the sights of South Delhi.

Ginger Hotel
MAP G5 ▪ IRCTC – Rail Yatra, New Delhi Railway Station, Bhav Bhutti Marg ▪ 6663 3333 ▪ www.gingerhotels.com ▪ ₹
Winner of the CNBC travel award for the Best Budget Hotel, this place has spotlessly clean rooms, a gym, Wi-Fi and a restaurant.

Hotel New Haven
MAP W2 ▪ E-512 Greater Kailash II ▪ 2921 8556 ▪ www.nhh.in ▪ ₹
This hotel has a good location in South Delhi and clean rooms. Guests can head to the nearby Greater Kailash market to choose from a variety of food options.

Hotel Tara Palace
MAP H4 ▪ 419 Esplanade Road, Chandni Chowk ▪ 2327 6465 ▪ www.tarapalacedelhi.com ▪ ₹
The good location and the friendly service compensate for the lacklustre look of the hotel. Set in the heart of Old Delhi, and with the Jama Masjid and Red Fort within walking distance, it makes it perfect for exploring this area.

International Youth Hostel
MAP K5 ▪ 5 Nyaya Marg, Chanakyapuri ▪ 2611 6285 ▪ www.yhaindia.org ▪ ₹
This is a huge favourite among young budget travellers for its location and facilities. Choose from a range of dorms, or double rooms with shared or private bathrooms.

Madpackers
MAP V2 ▪ 3rd floor, S–39A Panchsheel Park ▪ 98186 71874 ▪ ₹
Conveniently located close to a metro station, this informal hostel has dorms, including one just for women, making it a good choice for female travellers. There are plenty of communal spaces, including a kitchen and a terrace.

Metropolis Tourist Home
MAP F5 ▪ 1634, Main Bazar Road, Paharganj ▪ 2356 1782 ▪ www.metropolistouristhome.com ▪ ₹
Owing to its excellent location and friendly service, the Metropolis has fast become a popular budget option among backpackers. Located in the middle of busy Paharganj, it also has a great terrace restaurant.

Stops
MAP H5 ▪ 4/23-B Asaf Ali Road ▪ 4105 6226 ▪ www.stopshostels.com ▪ ₹
Join the backpacker crowd at this cool hostel on the southern edge of Old Delhi near Delhi Gate. There's a kitchen, bar, dorms and private rooms.

YMCA
MAP F7 ■ Jai Singh Road, Connaught Place ■ 2374 6031 ■ www.newdelhiymca.in/ndymcath ■ ₹

Since 1927, the YMCA hostel has provided excellent budget accommodation for foreign and local visitors. The rooms are basic but clean and have en-suite bathrooms. There is an Internet café and a restaurant serving traditional Indian food.

B&Bs and Guesthouses

Dawar Villa B&B
MAP G7 ■ 50 Todarmal Road, Bengali Market ■ 9911 321 555 ■ www.dawarvilla.com ■ ₹

This is a smart, family-run B&B located in Bengali Market, famous for its lively restaurants. Dawar Villa is also close to Mandi House, one of the city's main cultural centres. The place has a warm feel to it, with gorgeous wood panelling, earthy colours and soft lighting.

Delhi B&B
MAP X1 ■ A-6 Friends Colony (East) ■ 98110 57103 ■ www.delhibedandbreakfast.com ■ ₹

Boasting bright, quirky furniture, green potted plants and lovely wall-hangings, Delhi B&B is a pleasant place. Pervez and Lubna Hameed, the owners, are well travelled, speak fluent French and also offer advice on sightseeing in the city. Guests are welcome to watch the hostess prepare Indian meals.

Master Guesthouse
MAP B5 ■ R-500 New Rajendra Nagar ■ 2874 1089 ■ www.master-guesthouse.com ■ ₹

The family who run this beautifully kept little guesthouse are a mine of information on the city and their home is a delight. Breakfast is included and vegetarian meals are available.

On the House
MAP V1 ■ B-4/120 Safdarjung Enclave ■ 98110 47414 ■ www.bedandbreakfastnewdelhi.com ■ ₹

This B&B has seven rooms, named after trees, and each is decorated in vivid colours. It prides itself on its homely feel, and the home-cooked food here is delicious. It is a favourite with solo women travellers.

Sai Villa B&B
MAP W2 ■ E-578 Greater Kailash II ■ 98110 69943 ■ www.saivilla.com ■ ₹

It may not be the most stylish of guesthouses, but Sai Villa offers clean, spacious rooms, well-equipped, en-suite bathrooms, attentive staff and a prime location. The B&B also has deals with a number of nearby restaurants, so guests can ask to have meals delivered to their door.

Saket B&B
MAP V3 ■ 3rd Floor, D-21 Saket ■ 95828 72580 ■ www.saketbedandbreakfast.com ■ ₹

Located within a walking distance to the metro station and a short distance from Qutb Minar, Saket B&B is a comfortable option with spacious, well-maintained rooms and en-suite bathrooms. The popular malls Select Citywalk and DLF Place Saket are also easily accessible from here.

Tree of Life
MAP V3 ■ D-193 Saket ■ 98102 77699 ■ www.tree-of-life.in ■ ₹

There are seven spotless, spacious rooms, along with a lounge and kitchen, at this friendly little guesthouse in a quiet neighbourhood near the Qutb Minar, a short walk from Saket metro station.

Trendy B&B
MAP R7 ■ 9-B Mathura Road, Jangpura ■ 98993 54272 ■ www.trendybb.com ■ ₹

Run by a well-travelled owner with a network of friends across the globe, this B&B has something of a cosmopolitan feel. The rooms are spotlessly clean and spacious.

Vandana's B&B
MAP V1 ■ B-4/124 Safdarjung Enclave ■ 2618 6355 ■ www.bedandbreakfastnewdelhi.in ■ ₹

A warm, cosy family-run B&B, this boasts a charming rooftop garden, perfect for breakfast in the winter sun or a chilled drink in the summer.

11 Nizamuddin
MAP S6 ■ 11 Nizamuddin (East) ■ 98110 88966 ■ www.elevendelhi.com ■ ₹₹

Set in an elegant Colonial bungalow with a lawn, the rooms are charming, elegantly furnished and uncluttered. The area is smart, peaceful, quiet and close to several heritage monuments such as the grand Humayun's Tomb. There is a gym and a mini sports-complex nearby.

76 Friends Colony
MAP X1 ▪ 76 Friends Colony (West) ▪ 4145 4681 ▪ www.76friends colonywest.com ▪ ₹₹
This elegant B&B has cosy and well-ventilated rooms with basic amenities. The staff is friendly and helpful. Guests can relax in the lovely terrace garden.

G 49 Nizamuddin
MAP R6 ▪ G-49 Nizamuddin (West) ▪ 4737 3449 ▪ www.bed-breakfast.asia ▪ ₹₹
Tucked away in a leafy street, this is a relaxed, friendly place with elegant rooms and en-suite bathrooms. The dining area and balcony are lovely places to while away an evening.

Hotels Around Delhi

Tiger Den
MAP B3 ▪ Sariska, Alwar ▪ ₹
This state-run hotel is a great budget option for visitors to the Sariska Wildlife Sanctuary (see p73). Speak to the staff about sightseeing and safari tours in the park.

Diggi Palace
MAP B3 ▪ SMS Hospital Road, Jaipur ▪ 99290 92482 ▪ www.hotel diggipalace.com ▪ ₹₹
Built around 1727, Diggi Palace hosts a number of cultural events, including the annual Jaipur Literary Festival, which draws in writers from all over the globe. The hotel itself is

charming, with pretty fountains and rooms that hint at a glorious past.

Glasshouse on the Ganges
MAP C2 ▪ 23rd Milestone, Rishikesh–Badrinath Road, Gular–Dogi ▪ 09412 0764 20 ▪ www.glass house-on-the-ganges. neemranahotels.com ▪ ₹₹
Located in a fruit orchard, this hotel has six cottages overlooking the tumbling Ganges. Ask the staff about booking activities such as fishing, trekking and white-water rafting.

Hill Fort Kesroli
MAP B3 ▪ Kesroli, near MIS Post Office, Bahala, Alwar ▪ 98294 99901 ▪ www.the-hill-fort-kes roli.neemranahotels.com ▪ ₹₹
Set in an atmospheric 14th-century fort perched on a rocky outcrop, this charming little hotel offers splendid views of the surrounding mustard fields. The rooms are cool, with high ceilings, and are elegantly decorated in traditional style.

ITC Mughal
MAP C3 ▪ Taj Ganj, Agra ▪ 056 2402 1700 ▪ www. itcwelcomgroup.in ▪ ₹₹
This resort houses the country's largest spa. After a tiring day's sightseeing, relax in a private hammam (Turkish bath).

Kadamb Kunj
MAP C3 ▪ NH 11, Fatehpur Sikri, Bharatpur ▪ 05644 2201 22 ▪ www. kadambkunj.in ▪ ₹₹
Located not far from the Keoladeo Ghana National Park (see p72), the Kadam Kunj is very popular with birdwatchers.

Neemrana Fort-Palace
MAP B3 ▪ 122nd Milestone Delhi–Jaipur Highway, Neemrana, Alwar ▪ 01494 2460 07 ▪ www.fort-palace.neem ranahotels.com ▪ ₹₹
Carved into a hillside, this architectural jewel is steeped in history. Guests can try the pool, which offers amazing views of the countryside, or indulge in rejuvenating Ayurvedic spa treatments.

The Oberoi Amarvilas
MAP C3 ▪ Taj East Gate Road, Agra ▪ 0562 2231 515 ▪ www.amarvilas. com ▪ ₹₹₹
Constructed in a Moorish- and Mughal-inspired style, this gorgeous five-star property, not far from the Taj Mahal, is a beautiful place to stay.

Rambagh Palace
MAP B3 ▪ Bhawani Singh Road, Jaipur ▪ 0141 2385 700 ▪ www.tajhotels.com ▪ ₹₹₹
Built in 1835, Rambagh Palace was once the residence of Maharaja of Jaipur. An elegant air surrounds the lavish grounds of this property, also known as the "Jewel of Jaipur".

Tikli Bottom
MAP B3 ▪ Gairatpur Baas, PO Tikli, Gurugram ▪ 93133 70853 ▪ www. tiklibottom.com ▪ ₹₹₹
About an hour from Delhi lies this country hotel, owned by former British diplomats who stayed on after their posting in India. A Lutyens-style bungalow built around a courtyard, the house has a swimming pool and an organic farm.

For a key to hotel price categories see p114

General Index

Acknowledgments

The Authors
Gavin Thomas is a London-based travel writer specializing in the Gulf, Sri Lanka and, especially India. He is the author of *The Rough Guide to Dubai*, *The Rough Guide to Sri Lanka*, co-author of *The Rough Guide to Rajasthan, Delhi and Agra* and a contributing author to *The Rough Guide to India*.

Janice Pariat is a freelance writer based in Shillong. She has lived and worked in Delhi for almost a decade and loves the city's clash of culture, pace and climate. She writes travel stories for *HT City* (Mumbai) and *Travel to Care*, a website dedicated to eco-tourism.

Additional contributor
Daniel Jacobs

Publishing Director Georgina Dee
Publisher Vivien Antwi
Design Director Phil Ormerod
Editorial Ankita Awasthi Tröger, Michelle Crane, Dipika Dasgupta, Rachel Fox, Shikha Kulkarni, Maresa Manara, Ruth Reisenberger, Sally Schafer
Design Hansa Babra, Tessa Bindloss, Bharti Karakoti, Rahul Kumar, Ankita Sharma, Priyanka Thakur, Vinita Venugopal
Cover Design Richard Czapnik
Picture Research Subhadeep Biswas, Taiyaba Khatoon, Ellen Root, Rituraj Singh
Cartography Mohammad Hassan, Stuart James, Jasneet Kaur, Suresh Kumar, Casper Morris, Animesh Kumar Pathak
DTP Jason Little, George Nimmo, Azeem Siddiqui, Ajay Verma, Tanveer Zaidi
Production Jude Crozier
Factchecker Avantika Sukhia
Proofreader Clare Peel
Indexer Helen Peters
Commissioned Photography Idris Ahmed, Dinesh Khanna

Picture Credits

123RF.com: Sergey Belov 18bl; Lukasz Nowak 17crb; saiko3p 79cla.

Alamy Stock Photo: Arterra Picture Library 2tl, 2tr, 8-9, 40-1; Anders Blomqvist 32crb; Paul Springett C 20-1; dbimages 10cra, 26t, 34br, 69tr, 76tl, 99br; Deco 4t; epa european pressphoto agency b.v. 21bl; Hemis 3tr, 53br, 94br, 106-7; Angelo Hornak 32ca, 33tl, 33br; imageBROKER 4b, 61tr, 77tl; Inge Johnsson 4crb; Seth Lazar 27tr; Stelios Michael 49tr; William Mullins 4cla; David Pearson 13crb; PhotosIndia.com LLC 60ctb; Pictorial Press Ltd 43tl; Graham Prentice 22-3; robertharding 10b; Pep Roig 16bl; Clemente do Rosario 1; Tjetjep Rustandi 12-3; travelib prime 88cla; Emma Wood 4clb; Xinhua 71tr; ZUMA Press; Inc. 59tr.

Amrapali: 96ca.

Anokhi: 96b.

AWL Images: Gavin Hellier 55clb; Hemis 37crb; Nigel Pavitt 13tl, 90-1; Jane Sweeney 4cr.

Subhadeep Biswas: 11cr, 30cla, 30-1, 45cl.

Cafe Turtle: 103b.

Dreamstime.com: Stuart Atkinson 12bl, 39cb; Atosan 11tc, 66clb; Viacheslav Belyaev 84tl, 93tr; Ajay Bhaskar 78tl, 101cl; Byelikova 73b, 85b; Mike Clegg 10cla; Donyanedomam 38b; Elenatur 36-7; Euriico 80bl; Monica Furlong 11br; Jorg Hackemann 4cl, 10clb, 19crb, 47tr, 86cla; Icon72 10cb; Attila Jandi 73cra; Javiphotos 94t; Kajornyot 72c; Mdsindia 52br; Mvorobiev 50b; Moreno Novello 100b; Paweł Opaska 39t; William Perry 30crb; Marina Pissarova 56tl; Luca Roggero 57cl; Dmitry Rukhlenko 6cla; Saiko3p 16-7, 20bl, 36cla, 44b, 51t, 53t, 54t, 61b, 77br, 78b; Sergeychernov 46-7; Dr Ajay Kumar Singh 57tr; Singhsomendra 67tr; Pavalache Stelian 37tl; Rudolf Tepfenhart 38cla; Westhimal 7cra; Yuri Yavnik 7tr; Yurataranik 72tl, 98cla.

Fabindia: 102cr.

FIO Cookhouse and Bar: 105br.

Getty Images: Anadolu Agency 70t; Emad Aljumah 24-5, 85tr; Ulf Andersen 58tl; Mukul Banerjee Photography 3tl, 47clb, 74-5; Bettmann 43br; Anders Blomqvist 29bl; Bloomberg 104cb; Education Images 20cla; Hindustan Times 48t, 62t, 63bl; Angelo Hornak 11clb, 35bc, 42cr; IndiaPictures 32clb, 33bl, 35cl, 63tr; JUST LIKE THAT! 14br, 44tl, 88bc, 92cla; Ramesh Lalwani 54clb; Danny Lehman 67bl; Mail Today 97tr; Maremagnum 66tr; Mint 46b; Ashu Mittal 70bc; Pacific Press 62cb; Christine Pemberton 48bl; Christopher Pillitz 68br; Rhkamen 29tl; Smit Sandhir 27br; Mohan Singh 14cla, 15br; Frederic Soltan 51br; Leisa Tyler 65cla; Manan Vatsyayana 56-7; Visuals Unlimited; Inc. / Adam Jones 31tr.

iStockphoto.com: Jayesh 25clb; JDMaddox 31bc; Alan Lagadu 87tl; Meinzahn 18-9;